TEAC... ...ION

SEN... HIGH SCHOOL

By Samuel J. Rogal

About the Author

Samuel J. Rogal has taught junior and senior high school English in Reading and Coraopolis, Pennsylvania. He had positions on the faculties of Waynesburg College (as Coordinator of Freshman Composition), Iowa State University, and taught in the Pre-Freshman English Program at Tuskegee Institute. Beginning September, 1966, Mr. Rogal will become Director of Freshman English at the State University College, Oswego, New York. He has authored ten articles on high school and college composition, and is currently a member of an authorship team preparing a high school linguistics-composition series.

About the Book

1. TEACHING COMPOSITION IN THE SENIOR HIGH SCHOOL was written to clarify the aims of composition for college students preparing to teach English in the high school and in-service teachers of high school English.

2. The author's basic philosophy is that composition is the most important program in the high school curriculum.

3. The book is designed as a manual to encompass all facets of the teacher's responsibility in the composition program — from selecting texts to reading themes.

4. The most comprehensive section, extremely valuable for beginning teachers, presents a step-by-step process for reading student themes.

5. Included are over forty sample theme topics.

6. A separate section contains ten themes, transcribed in the original, for the reader to criticize and correct.

808.042
R63t

TEACHING COMPOSITION
IN THE
SENIOR HIGH SCHOOL

by
Samuel J. Rogal
Director of Freshman English
State University College, Oswego, New York

1966

LITTLEFIELD, ADAMS & CO.
Totowa, New Jersey

Copyright © 1966
LITTLEFIELD ADAMS CO.

Library of Congress catalog card No. 66-18143

Printed in the United States of America

TEACHING COMPOSITION
IN THE
SENIOR HIGH SCHOOL

By Samuel J. Rogal

CONTENTS

Introduction:	The Purpose of the High School Composition Program	ix
SECTION I:	Selection of Texts	
	1. Minimum Requirements	3
	2. The Reading Anthology for the High School Composition Program	5
	3. Responsibility for Selection	7
SECTION II:	The Organization of the High School Composition Program	
	1. The Need for Thoughtful Planning	13
	2. The Mechanics of Organization ..	14
	3. Suggested Minimum Requirements	15
	4. Explanation of the Minimum Requirements	18
	5. The Need for Flexibility	19
SECTION III:	The Role of Grammar	
	1. The Problems of Grammar	23
	2. Grammar as an Aid to Language in Action	26
SECTION IV:	Organization, Transition, and Development: Essentials for Writing and Thinking	
	1. The Need for Organization, Transition, and Development	31
	2. The Guiding Purpose	32
	3. The Theme Plan	33
	4. Transition	35
	5. Development	37
	6. The Importance of Teaching Organization, Transition, and Development	39

SECTION V:	Topics for Students' Themes	
	1. The Teacher's Responsibility	43
	2. The Results of Inexperience	44
	3. What Constitutes a Legitimate Writing Assignment	46
	4. The Need to "Know Your Students"	47
	5. Specific Topics for Student Themes	50
	6. More Formal Writing Projects	53
SECTION VI:	Reading the Theme	
	1. The Reading Process	57
	2. A Sample Theme to Illustrate the Reading Process	59
	3. Stage 1: The Guiding Purpose	60
	4. Stage 2: The Outline	61
	5. Stage 3: The First Reading	62
	6. Stage 4: The Second Reading	63
	7. Stage 5: The Third Reading	64
	8. Stage 6: The Fourth Reading	68
	9. Stage 7: The Final Evaluation	74
SECTION VII:	Revisions and Re-Writings	75
SECTION VIII:	Sample Themes for Practice	
	1. A Note on the Sample Themes	83
	2. Narrative	83
	3. Exposition	93
	4. The Book Review	109
SECTION IX:	Composition and Literature: Maintaining a SENSIBLE Balance	
	1. The Role of Literature in the High School Composition Program	115
	2. Critical Writing	117
	3. What High School Literature is NOT	119
	4. Suggestions for Maintaining a Sensible Balance	123
SECTION X:	A Selected Reading List for the Teaching of High School Composition	127
SECTION XI:	The Future of the High School Composition Program	133

INTRODUCTION

The Purpose of the High School Composition Program

A large high school in western Pennsylvania has as its motto the phrase "Know Something, Do Something, Be Something." These six words are prominently displayed, yet the majority of students who walk the halls of this school find the message to be superfluous; they do not need to be reminded that learning, in order to have meaning for themselves and the society of which they will soon become an active part, must be put to good and practical *use*. For them the only problem is time. They are anxious to apply the acquired knowledge and some find difficulty in learning to wait until graduation before they can "Know, Do, Be." So off they rush to the chemistry lab or the machine shop, where the bubbling of test tubes and the whirring of motors keeps pace, in their world, with the rush of the adult society to produce bigger and better things. Today they learn, tomorrow—in the lab or shop—they do; it is as simple as that!

But not every high school course can be so easily adapted or transferred to the laboratory next door. Realizing this, administrators press their faculties to the whipping post of practical application: cookies roll from the ovens of the home economics department; history and geography teachers emerge from closed conferences, and the next day eager hands chart old states and trails on newly mimeographed maps; biology students label very tree in the neighborhood; and the art and music departments exhibit visually, orally, and respectively every other week.

Yet somehow, through this vast maze of physical activity, the most obvious—and the most practical—method for putting knowledge to work has been ignored: that communicating this new-found knowledge to others can provide students with conditions similar to those in the science lab or manual arts shop. Truly, the communication of ideas—the transfer of knowledge from the learner to the uninitiated—is the quickest, most efficient manner by which young and eager minds can apply their learning.

There are only two methods, of course, by which the student can communicate: oral or written. Of the two, written communication is the more exciting, if for no other reason than it is permanent. Also, the fact that it is a highly developed skill should present a challenge to the alert young minds of the "sixties." For writing is no different from a delicate craft that requires years of training or apprenticeship before the neophyte can be trusted to perform efficiently. Nor is it different from the sport that requires its participants to undergo constant conditioning, often at varying degrees of competition, before they become "stars." But in most cases, this skill is more difficult to master than any that the student has heretofore attempted. It requires years of practice and patience, entwined with periods of utter frustration, before an individual can master the discipline of writing correctly. Often, the writing student cannot project himself sufficiently into the future in order to see the necessity for this skill; more often, upon reaching maturity, he discovers his dearly bought skill lying dormant for some time, and when called upon, it fails him because idleness has weakened those once finely wrought tools of written communication. So this difficulty can easily bring about an attitude of indifference on the part of the high school student which, if allowed to continue, may lead to the complete neglect of one of the most important skills that an individual needs to attain.

Therefore, the teaching of writing is the most valuable program in the secondary school curriculum. As far as the student's entire education is concerned, his ability to write represents the most workable tool for every other academic discipline, and it reflects the individual's ability to think, organize, and create. No other skill can require so much from a student and likewise demand that he produce a permanent record that furnishes ample evidence as to whether or not he has successfully met those requirements. For this reason, the ability to produce clear, well-organized, and disciplined prose is an absolute necessity in practically every profession and vocation.

With this in mind, the teacher of English is blessed with the responsibility for implanting, then cultivating, this skill in his students. And it is not necessary to dwell upon the fact that his position in the school system and the community that it serves is commensurate with the importance of the composition program in the high school curriculum. For every young person, no matter how great or small is his native ability, is complete with experiences which he desires to share with others. Therefore, since the motivation for communication is inherent within him, no student is at a loss for material, especially when ideas come easily to the alert and eager mind. In the majority of instances, the only avenue for the expression of these ideas and experiences is the high school composition program, and the teacher of writing is failing himself, his students, and the profession he represents if he fails to keep these avenues widely open. The teacher who does not provide his students with adequate opportunities to write, who devotes the major portion of the program to areas not essential to the development of the fundamentals of disciplined writing, who does not encourage his students to express themselves through the medium of the written word, or who is not conscientious in assisting his students to improve beyond the mere fundamentals of language skills is nothing short of incompetent.

The purpose of the high school composition program, then, is clear: to provide a training ground where young minds will be able to assimilate the essential writing skills and students will receive as much practice as possible preparatory to entering a vocation or an institution of higher education. If educators begin to realize that this program can function smoothly with only this simple but practical goal and a competent teaching staff, then the high school English departments of this nation will begin to produce disciplined student-writers.

The composition program does not exist for the purpose of training potential writers of the great American novel, but to prepare young people to meet the qualifications of a basic communications skill that will be required in almost every facet of their adult lives. This involves two areas of concentration: to provide the non-academic student with the opportunity to advance in his chosen vocation and to prepare the college-bound student for the requirements of the freshman English program, which is the final step before he applies his skill to the highly complex and demanding profession of his choice. Whether or not the composition program is to be organized on such distinct levels as these is arguable; of primary importance is that unless the program can provide the student with the ability "to project reasonably" a unified idea, written in a clear, disciplined manner, the entire English curriculum might as well be eliminated from secondary education.

Section I

SELECTION OF TEXTS

1. Minimum Requirements
2. The Reading Anthology for the Composition Program
3. Responsibilities for Selection

1. Minimum Requirements

The number of textbooks now available for the teaching of composition is so numerous that to arrive at a possible evaluation on the merits or limits of each is impossible. Since the purpose of this section is not to serve as a clearing house for publishers of high school English texts—the avalanche of brochures and advertising circulars descending almost daily upon English teachers will accomplish this—there remains only to consider and to establish what constitutes a good text, no matter whom the author or publisher. Thus, a discussion of what *should* constitute a worthwhile text will prove helpful if it does nothing else but suggest that the quality of the material rise to the level of the quantity. Although the composition program is of prime consideration in this manual, nevertheless a discussion of high school literature anthologies is necessary, since the works of established authors are an integral part of the writing program.

Of all the composition texts currently on the market, that which is published in handbook format is perhaps the most convenient for both teacher and student. A good handbook will contain only the material that is absolutely necessary for the conduct of a practical composition program. Also, its size and arrangement provide easy access to individual trouble areas, which is especially helpful because not everyone has difficulty with the same problem. Too often texts are weighted down with the likes of trying to explain to the student why he is studying English (a fact that he ought to know if the teacher and the overall purpose of the composition program are worth anything); materials dealing with oral communication—discussions, debates, symposiums, parliamentary procedure—which really belong in a separate speech course; or sections about literary genres. Albeit these matters are important to a student's complete education, but a text that attempts to discuss *everything* becomes difficult to adopt in a course that emphasizes one particular skill. The purpose of the high school composition text should be to assist the student in increasing his writing ability, and if the material is not easily accessible—if it is buried among piles of irrelevancies—then the book becomes a hindrance and is quickly cast aside in disgust. Finally, the handbook allows the qualified teacher greater freedom because his teaching is not confined to teaching all of the material in a given text during the entire year. It also forces the incompetent teacher to get out from under the covers of the text and apply his own ingenuity (providing that this is possible) in assisting his students to become better writers.

Perhaps the best handbook now in use at both the high school and college levels is divided into numbered sections, each referring to a principle in grammar, mechanics, punctuation, or the elements of the composition. The size of the text is approximately seven and one-quarter inches by four and three-quarter inches, and it contains slightly over five hundred pages. Although the size, and consequently the cost, is convenient, the advantage lies with these numbered sections that facilitate the location of a particular problem by the student. Therefore, the teacher can point to the exact section in the text where the student can locate a corrected version of a particular theme error.

But no matter what text is to be recommended for the composition program, it ought to contain chapters or sections based upon the following minimum requirements:

1. *Modern* grammatical principles
2. Mechanics
3. Spelling
4. Punctuation
5. Diction: to include a modern glossary of usage, with the levels clearly marked
6. Types of sentences and their correct handling within the paragraph
7. Organization: to include the plan for the paragraph and the full length composition
8. Transition
9. Development

10. The elements of the composition
    a. The paragraph
    b. The full length composition
    c. The research paper: to include documentation
11. Letters
    a. Business
    b. Application for employment
    c. Social

All of the above items are basic to the teaching of practical writing, yet they should be stated as clearly as possible in order that the student will not be too dependent upon his teacher for reviewing the material in a particular area. Unless classes are grouped in strict order of ability, it will be extremely difficult for the composition teacher to transport simultaneously the entire class from one skill level to the next. Therefore, those who are able to advance with greater rapidity should be permitted to do so, and they will be aided substantially if textual material is sufficiently clear and constructive of its suggestions to allow independent study. Still, an accompanying workbook would be helpful, providing the text itself does not contain exercises for practice in the more difficult aspects of grammar and mechanics. There will have to be a certain amount of drill, especially during the freshman year (grade nine), on points in which the majority of students is having difficulty. Drill in grammar and mechanics is valid if the themes show evidence that it is needed, but these exercises become a complete waste of time if employed without reason in areas in which the students display adequate understanding.

2. The Reading Anthology for the Composition Program

Regarding an accompanying reading anthology for the composition program, the problem of selection is much simpler than that of the writing text. Although there are just as many, if not more, anthologies on the market as there are composition texts, the only difference among the former is the ease by which they can be adapted to the entire composition program. The primary purpose of the anthology is to inspire the student with new ideas for his own compositions and enable him to observe the effectiveness of the techniques and methods of professional writers. This last objective is most important, since the student-writer who is able to sharpen his critical judgment to see both the good and poor aspects of a published essay is preparing himself for the more vital role of criticizing his own writing to the point where he will be self-confident to judge *its* assets and liabilities.

Naturally, the selection of a specific literature or reading anthology depends upon several factors. First, consideration must be given to the specific grade level in which the text will be employed; second, it would be wise to consider the intentions of students in regard to interests in school and aims after graduation—for instance, college preparatory students will require different reading backgrounds from those who are preparing for non-academic vocations. Finally, the anthology should parallel the aims of the school curricula, especially the objectives of the entire English program. Is the emphasis to be placed on American or English literature; upon world literature or literary forms, without any special consideration as to period or nationality? No matter what the emphasis, the selection of an appropriate literature or reading anthology is never difficult as long as those responsible for selection know exactly what they are to do with the text after it has been adopted.

Since the teaching of literature should never be divorced from the teaching of composition, the text that is finally selected should contain questions on the form, style and content of each work, in addition to some good suggestions for composition topics. Teachers must never forget that in most cases, these poems, essays, novels, or plays were not written for high school students, and any help that the text and the instructor can provide for the young reader will naturally make the work more meaningful to him. Editors of anthologies usually realize that their texts will be used in connection with the writing of compositions, and often the selections are categorized by types to facilitate recognition by the student.

What is strongly suggested here is that the reading anthology that is assembled with the composition program in mind is preferable to that which is dedicated to a rather close study of literature, where reading takes precedence over writing.

3. Responsibility for Selection

The consideration of the text for the composition program, either the writing text or the reading anthology, presents only a minor problem when contrasted to the utter chaos that exists over where the responsibility lies in making the actual selection. This is not really a separate matter in itself, but merely an extension of the shoddy inefficiency predominant in too many English departments at the high school level: lack of qualified teachers, no administration of the course, unworkable or nonexistent courses of study, and no coordination within the department or with the school administration. In other words, the philosophy of "anything goes" accompanies the cry of "anyone can teach English," and the result is that, at the end of the year, NO ONE CAN WRITE! No wonder, then, that a procedure as simple as the selection of a textbook or two becomes almost a battle for power. But this battle, and the possible war that might ensue, can be avoided if and when teachers and administrators begin to apply logic instead of the brute force of authority. Within any academic department, the decision for selecting texts for required courses—and in the high school just about everything is required—should be made at one of three levels, presented here in the order of preference.

The greatest satisfaction would certainly arise from the decisions of the entire teaching staff of the English department after a thorough examination of a wide variety of text books. Of course there will always be differences of opinion, and not all members will be satisfied. But the final selection will have been the result of a majority, which is always the first step toward unification and coöperation within the program. If a decision cannot be reached at this level, the next best area would be one handed down by a special committee on the selection of textbooks. This group would be comprised of department members selected by the chairman or senior teacher in charge. However, care should be taken to insure that this committee change from year to year—or whenever new texts are to be selected—so that each member of the staff knows that he still has an opportunity to be heard before the final decision is made. The advantage here is that a smaller group can often accomplish what a large, sometimes highly divided assemblage cannot. Finally, if this committee cannot fulfill its purpose, the only alternative is for the department chairman to make the decision himself. Although there can be worse areas of responsibility in this matter, an arbitrary judgment by an individual is not the best, since there are always teachers who will disagree to the point that they might become almost insubordinate. This is a natural reaction, since professional people dislike being told what to do without having first been consulted. Yet, if the department chairman is a qualified and competent teacher of English, his selection will most likely leave no room for violent dissent and criticism.

However, there are certain of the above individuals or groups in this category who should not be responsible for selection. Since seniority is held in esteem by too many administrators and faculty members, there is a tendency to place only "veteran" teachers on committees that are concerned with important matters of academic policy. The dangers of having texts continually selected by senior teachers are obvious: the conservative point of view, which often accompanies a long term of service, might dominate the committee's attitude and bring about the adoption of a stern prescriptive text; this text, and perhaps the entire composition program, could present an intense conflict with modern trends in the teaching of writing; and a text selected by senior staff members is likely to be rejected by younger teachers, causing a decided breach in both the department and the organization of the composition program.

Yet a selection committee comprised only of junior members of the English faculty will create the same situation in reverse. Too often young teachers are obsessed with the notion that "anything goes" in language and writing, and what is good for Salinger, Eliot, Pound, and Kerouac is suitable for a ninth grade English class. Whenever balance is taken from a group vested with responsibility, the result will be a decision based only upon the particular likes and dislikes of the individuals who decide. The English language and the high school composition program have not yet arrived to the point where the new can be separated from the old. Since both have definite advantages and disadvantages to the young student learning the sensitive skill of written communication, he must be aided by teachers and materials that will incorporate only the advantages of each.

Section II

THE ORGANIZATION OF THE HIGH SCHOOL COMPOSITION PROGRAM

1. The Need for Thoughtful Planning
2. The Mechanics of Organization
3. Suggested Minimum Requirements
4. Explanation of the Minimum Requirements
5. The Need for Flexibility

1. The Need for Thoughtful Planning

A specific purpose, specially trained teachers, and practical textbooks become impotent tools if the high school composition program is not held together by a workable yet flexible organizational plan. The need for organization within the writing program is apparent when one considers the complete subjectivity of a skill such as writing: the involvement of ideas, the direction of these ideas toward a single theme, the subsequent communication of this theme to a reading audience, and the final criticism of its function as an adequate instrument of communication. Because all of these components of an individual's skill as a writer are in a continual state of suspension until he can master sufficient discipline to bring them simultaneously into action suggests that only through uniformity in methods of procedure can the composition program become successful in dispensing needed assistance toward the mastery of this discipline.

Progress in any skill depends upon individual ability, and it is often difficult to see clearly ahead to the time when the instructor can declare that his protégé has become an accomplished practitioner. In other words, the lines marked "Start" and "Finish" are not drawn: the freshman quarterback might make the varsity and bask in glory for four years; perhaps he might require three years of constant conditioning on the practice field until, as a senior, he finally breaks into the starting line-up. Transferred to the English class, this analogy changes only as it is applied to a different skill: many students enter the ninth grade lacking merely maturity and a fully developed vocabulary to make them disciplined or exceptional writers; others must practice almost until they graduate before the ability to write disciplined prose asserts itself; others, like many would-be athletes, never make the varsity.

Only careful planning on the part of competent English teachers will provide the assurance that *every* student will become endowed with the ability to make the team—in this case, the ability to write *disciplined* prose that will communicate a unified idea, and the *gifted* student will advance toward the difficult subjective type based on his own opinions and ideas, on perception and imagination. The composition program that leaves a great deal to chance, that goes no further than to stress the fundamentals of language structure, or that turns its objectives away from the teaching of writing is a sham. The only program that can hope to succeed in its objective of teaching high school students the principles of correct writing is the one that has been thoughtfully planned to carry these students through a sustained procedure of training in composition throughout their four years in the secondary school. As far as extending beyond this purpose—to develop writing skills along creative or technical lines—the composition teacher has the responsibility for judging just how far he can advance a class or an individual *after* the minimum writing requirements have been satisfied.

2. The Mechanics of Organization

Actually, there are three possible sources, all of them reliable, for the planning of a course of study for the composition program. For a start, there is the department chairman or senior teacher in charge of the English staff, providing the staff is organized in this manner. Assuming that this individual received his appointment as a result of his qualifications and ability as a teacher of writing, his program must assuredly be accepted as valid by the entire staff out of respect for his competency. Presumably, there will be differences of opinion, but if they are sound criticisms, they can very easily be taken into consideration in the outlining of the program. Should the English department be without a chairman, the program can then be planned by a revolving committee on organization and content, which would work in close association with the entire staff. A revolving committee should function smoothly, since every member of the staff will sometime or other be able to make an active contribution toward the improvement of the entire program. Finally, there is the possibility of the composition program being organized by the entire staff, providing, of course, it is not so large as to be impractical as a workable unit. But the program can only be *organized* by the entire staff; supervision will have to be the responsibility of a qualified individual or a small, revolving committee. A department chairman or a representative committee can adequately enforce the program that has been adopted, but an entire teaching staff cannot very well police itself.

In the final analysis, then, the composition program that is successful is also the one that has been authored by members of the *teaching* staff. Administrators, especially those who are well qualified in curriculum planning, should be permitted to contribute worthwhile suggestions, but the greatest responsibility must be placed in the hands of those who are closest to the program.

3. Suggested Minimum Requirements

Outlined below are recommended *minimum* essentials to provide a student with the ability to write a clearly understood theme. This plan is not intended as a complete course of study for four years of high school English; it is only a starting point from which the program can be broadened in scope or limited, depending upon the aims and abilities of the students. The plan also assumes that in order to be successful in meeting the writing requirements of the senior high school, the student must be equipped with a working knowledge of the English language—and this means the fundamentals of grammar—in the seventh and eighth grades. Finally, the outline contains only the writing portion of the composition;

the teaching of literature and its function within the program are discussed in SECTION IX.

The Composition Program By Grades
Suggested Minimum Requirements

Grade Nine:
1. Review as *needed*:
   a. Grammar
   b. Punctuation
   c. Mechanics
   d. Spelling
2. The word: emphasis upon variety and concrete detail
3. Vocabulary study
4. The sentence
   a. Types
   b. Sentence Variety
5. Selecting and limiting the theme topic
6. Organizing the theme idea: the paragraph plan (outline)
   a. Types of outlines
   b. Controlling the topic through the Guiding Purpose (See SECTION IV, 2)
7. The paragraph
   a. The topic sentence
   b. Supporting details
   c. Concluding sentence
   d. Methods of paragraph development
   e. Sentence transition within the pararaph
8. Expanding the paragraph to a complete composition
   a. Introductory paragraph
   b. Concluding paragraph
   c. Developing the body of the composition
   d. Organization of the entire composition
   e. Paragraph transition within the composition
   f. Selecting and limiting the subject
9. Time to be equally divided between the personal narrative and exposition

Grade Ten:
1. Review of paragraph essentials *as needed*
   a. Topic sentence
   b. Supporting details

    c. Concluding sentence
    d. Paragraph development
    e. Sentence transition
    f. Organization
2. Time to be equally divided between the personal narrative and exposition
3. Selecting and limiting the subject for the longer composition
4. Continued emphasis upon the following areas of the complete composition:
    a. Organization
    b. Development
    c. Transition
5. Continued vocabulary study
6. Stimulation of ideas through readings of noted writers, both past and present
    a. Book reviews
    b. Short, critical papers

Grade Eleven:
1. Personal narratives may continue as a start, but students should be brought to the point where they can venture outside of their own experiences and begin to explore new topics for communication through writing:
    a. Ideas from the writings of others (literature)
    b. Ideas from other academic disciplines
2. Continued vocabulary study
3. Continued emphasis on organization and transition
4. Any previous limits on the length of papers should be removed and extended to the writer's ability to handle the assigned topic (and the teacher's ability to read it, along with some 125-150 others per week)
5. Instruction on methods and materials of research
6. *Short* research papers

Grade Twelve:
1. Papers of unlimited length
2. Emphasis upon expository writing, with personal narratives for variety
3. Vocabulary study
4. Organization, transition, and development of the long research paper
5. More intensified instruction on the methods and materials of research.

4. Explanation of the Minimum Requirements

Anticipating some of the criticisms that might be directed toward the preceding plan, an explanation of its more obvious intentions is in order. First, the program is repetitive in places—intentionally so. For example, Grade Ten repeats, to a degree, the essentials of the paragraph that were emphasized in Grade Nine, in addition to organization, development, and transition of both the single paragraph and the whole composition. Also, the areas of organization, transition, and development are repeated in Grades Eleven and Twelve. The justification for this is that these three elements of writing provide students with most of their difficulties, and each theme or paragraph presents a distinct problem in organization, transition, and development. Therefore, these items are reemphasized, rather than merely repeated; they are constantly persented in different forms, depending upon the type of composition that the student is writing and the specific topic that is to be discussed.

Second, Grade Ten is more of an extension of Grade Nine then a separate entity. The reason is that the development of a student's writing skill is a unified process—like the smooth flow of a river—and this process cannot be divided as easily as the grade divisions in the secondary schools. In other words, the first two years of the composition program represent the period when the basic essentials of the skill are implanted, while the last two become the period wherein the student practices and extends these fundamentals to larger, more complex writing problems. The high school composition program should at least exist on these two levels, but further partition can easily be accomplished to meet the administrative needs of the school and the abilities of the students. Flexibility is the byword of this program, and this topic will be considered in detail in the following subsection.

Finally, a word concerning the vocabulary study, which is included at every grade level. Detailed explanation is unnecessary, since everyone is aware that a student's writing must mature with his mind. It is essential to all forms of communication that a young person build a "powerful" (to use the commercial term) vocabulary to facilitate the ease by which his oral and written ideas can be transmitted. In writing, the student who has a large vocabulary at his command, and who knows what to do with it, will discover that his sentences are clear and concise; therefore, his entire composition is easily assimilated by the reader.

Two areas of the composition program have been omitted from this plan, but intentionally so. The actual writing assignments—type, number, and criticism of—are discussed in SECTIONS V and VI. Library study, and the various projects that usually accompany it, has been excluded because by now this has become almost a ritual in high school English classes. More and more librarians are becoming teachers of a highly technical and academic subject; the image of file clerks armed with rubber stamps and dust cloths has been destroyed, and the library is perhaps the most essential part of a student's education. However, it is also the most expensive, and the quality and quantity of library study in the senior high school depends upon the financial resources of the school to determine whether or not the students are provided with an adequate library and a competent staff to maintain it. But if college preparatory students are to be efficiently trained in the methods and materials of research writing, school libraries will have to be provided with adequate finances to meet this requirement.

5. The Need for Flexibility

In arriving at the final evaluation of any recommended coherent and constructive program for the teaching of composition at the high school level, the most important topic to be considered is that of its flexibility. Any course of study must always be based upon the need for flexibility within the program, especially since the American system of public education has no central governing body. Because, for all intents and purposes, every school district has practically a free hand in the selection of staff members and the formation of curricula, the content of each academic discipline is dependent upon two factors, each relevant to the high school composition program.

The first is the quality of the English teachers in a particular school; the second is the quality of the students. The individual or committee responsible for organizing the composition program must always consider these two before the program can become operational. A rigid program could possibly be effective if, for example, the school has on its faculty only well-trained and competent English teachers instructing students who are relatively equal in writing ability and who have similar aims after graduation. But there are few high schools—if any at all—where this situation exists. For the most part, English departments are staffed by a cosmopolitan group: the old and the young, the trained and the untrained, the competent and the incompetent, the conscientious and the habitual malingerers. The desires and abilities of students are even more diverse, and the attempts to categorize teenagers according to what they want to "be" when they graduate or segregate them on the basis of what they can "do" while they are in school have never resulted in anything conclusive. Consequently, the composition program *must* be flexible—it must bend and turn and twist to meet every need and classroom situation; it must be revised periodically to eliminate apparent superfluities and to contend with new problems; and it must constantly be studied and tried and studied again until a workable program is achieved.

In concluding this chapter, it must be stressed—as can be observed at a glance from the outline in Subsection 3—that two basic alternatives are clearly evident: If the fundamentals of writing are firmly implanted within the first two years of the student's training, then the last two permit the teacher to review thoroughly and thus be sure that his students have at least grasped the minimum essentials of their skill. Or, this skill can be advanced as far as the teacher's time and the abilities of the class will allow.

Section III

THE ROLE OF GRAMMAR

1. The Problems of Grammar
2. Grammar as an Aid to Language in Action

1. The Problems of Grammar

When forming langauge habits, young people of high school age are most influenced by their families and friends; in other words, by those people with whom they have the closest contacts. If these individuals themselves possess language habits that can be classified as reasonably "proper," the high school English teacher discovers that his task of teaching "correct" English is relatively simple, and he can then concentrate his efforts upon helping the students put their language to work as they perfect their communications skills through the writing of compositions. However, if language habits are loosely and improperly formed, then a great deal of time will have to be devoted to the instruction of more "correct" usage. This all appears as a rather clear and logical plan for the teacher of English: after first determining his students' needs, he will act accordingly; grammar is emphasized before any writing is attempted, or the program begins immediately with the writing of themes on the assumption that the students possess a sufficient knowledge of language fundamentals. Unfortunately, the problem of how or when to integrate the study of English essentials with the composition program cannot be disposed of with such relative ease. Two factors prevent this.

In the first place, the major portion of the composition program, especially during the initial two years, will be devoted to informal, personal expression. Students will be asked to communicate their experiences and observations to the reader, and in order to create an atmosphere of genuine reality, the language must combine discipline with ease of expression. The teacher who leans toward the principles of traditional grammar will discover that his students' compositions might reverberate with grammatical correctness, but they will lack the "live" quality of style that so characterizes the teenager of the 1960's. Yet the same can be said for the opposite point of view. The teacher who believes that correctness in language terminated with the passing of the eighteenth century will be rudely awakened to observe that his student-writers are so free with their language as to be almost totally incapable of communicating their ideas so that someone can understand them. Clearly, a compromise must be found, but here lies the second factor preventing an agreeable solution to the problem of grammar within the composition program.

The teacher who looks upon the concepts of traditional grammar as the sole authority for correctness in writing has the least difficulty in solving this problem. In his mind, students are writing correctly—and will continue to do so—when they adhere to the numerous rules and definitions that have been in vogue since the ages of Dionysius Thrax and Quintillian. But the English teacher who advocates the modern approach, namely that usage establishes correctness in language cannot accept this. In parrying the dogmas of his more traditional colleagues, he wants the answers to some questions: Who is to be responsible for determining the criteria for "proper" or "correct" language that will determine the degree of emphasis to be placed on grammar during the conduct of the composition program? Will the language of the community that surrounds the school and provides it with subsistence be accepted by the school as "proper"? Is the administration responsible for determining how the student population will speak and write, as well as how they will dress and what they will eat for lunch? Or, does determining correctness in language rest with a majority of the members of the English staff? Obviously, an English department can become totally involved in this controversy over how the essentials of the language can best be dispensed to the students; in fact many a principal or department chairman finds himself trying desperately to appease with more or less success both factions in an effort to maintain harmony within the staff and throughout the entire composition program. Each concept has its own particular merits when observed from an isolated point of view, but teachers must remember that to teach a language—*any* language—is a waste of time unless it can be put to use.

This is not to say that English grammar, with its traditional terms and definitions, should be banished from the primary and secondary schools of the United States. Granted, this would solve the entire matter, but unfortunately it would then create newer and probably more complex dilemmas. Just as with everything else in this world—from communism to racial prejudice—the only answer lies in education. When any large controversy or differences of opinion occur, the educator has the responsibility of presenting every aspect of the problem from every possible standpoint. It is hardly conceivable that students and teachers can understand the concepts of the so-called "new" grammar (descriptive linguistics and transformational grammar, for example) unless they are familiar with the more traditional forms of the English language and the problems arising from them, which provoked this controversy in the first place. But this enlightenment should occur early in the student's education so that he can devote the major portion of his high school English activities to the need for becoming more proficient in the area of written communication. English supervisors at the elementary level might well consider greater concentration on the English language; not only emphasis upon traditional and modern grammatical principles, but a thorough study of the history of the English language as well.

But no matter at *what* level it is taught, isolated grammar—be it either the new or traditional concept—has no place in the high school composition program. Older and more conservative teachers of English have long held to the opinion that before a student can learn to write in a clear and concise manner, he must *first* be led through a labyrinth of grammatical hodgepodge that is complete with rules, definitions, conjugations, declensions, parses, diagrams, and drills. The old adage that a carpenter needs tools before he can practice his craft has become tiresome, if not altogether impractical. For when the native speaker of English reaches his fourteenth or fifteenth year, he has, in most instances, a complete set of tools; all that is required is that they be sharpened and then utilized. The only advantage—if indeed it is an advantage at all—to teaching isolated grammar is that it provides an easy way to organize an English course; the class studies the noun on September first and terminates the school year sometime in June by diagramming the first sentence of the Declaration of Independence. In this manner, so much attention has been devoted to blueprints and tools that suddenly there is not sufficient time remaining for the actual construction of the edifice—the all important composition skill.

2. Grammar as an Aid to Language in Action

There is absolutely no reason why a student cannot become familiar with the intricacies of the English language while he is using it. This is truly language in action. The really valuable and therefore practical composition program will take full advantage of student themes as a basis for the amount of grammar to be taught during a four year period. For example, if a teacher discovers that the most recent collection of themes contains a sufficient number of errors in subject-verb agreement, the very next class hour should be devoted to an explanation and discussion of the principles governing correctness in this area. Or, if only a small minority of students is having difficulty with this problem, then individual drill work assigned to them—and to them only—should prove helpful toward an understanding and eventual elimination of the error. What is being advocated here is that if students are not making errors in particular areas of grammar, then why bother teaching that which, according to the composition, is thoroughly understood?

From another point of view, that of the teacher, the method of allowing the written compositions to determine the amount of grammar to be taught forces the English faculty toward a greater awareness of student writing and, more important, of the most recent language trends. As a result, the students can concentrate the major portion of their English training on perfecting their writing skills. In this manner, they can join their teachers in developing a disciplined, yet modern concept of language correctness.

The elimination of isolated grammar from the composition program will concurrently aid in further eliminating much of the useless objectivity from the entire English curriculum and, perhaps, even from secondary education itself, where objectivity runs rampant. Too often teachers are instructed to administer daily quizzes, weekly chapter tests, unit tests, and final examinations. Then, when the scores are tabulated and entered in the grade book, Mrs. Jones can *see* that her son failed English; even *she* can comprehend that a total of 45 points out of a possible 500 is not very good achievement! But show her Johnny's final composition, a paper that proves beyond doubt that the boy needs another year of sophomore English to practice his writing skill at that level, and she will argue all the way to the school board that one paper *cannot* determine a final grade.

If the English teacher is forced to submit to a bevy of daily, weekly, and monthly tests throughout the composition program, then grammar and other irrelevant material will out of necessity weigh more than the most important product—the written theme. Yet this is happening every academic term because supposed educators fail to understand that writing is a skill that demands four years of constant practice on the part of high school students; it is not merely another *course* where a grade can be determined by the flick of a percentile or the twist of a bell-shaped curve. The student's grade, and therefore the subsequent advancement of his writing skill, should be determined by his ability to write good, disciplined prose, not by the number of verbs he can conjugate or the sentences he can diagram.

Section IV

ORGANIZATION, TRANSITION, AND DEVELOPMENT: ESSENTIALS FOR WRITING AND THINKING

1. The Need for Organization, Transition, and Development
2. The Guiding Purpose
3. The Theme Plan
4. Transition
5. Development
6. The Importance of Teaching Organization, Transition, and Development

1. The Need for Organization, Transition, and Development

Perhaps the best possible motivation that the teacher of high school English can employ in the composition program is to propound the principle that the rigor of perfecting the skill of effective written communication is not an end in itself; nor is the theme that shows the results of this skill. Students must, first of all, be made to realize that writing is dependent upon thinking, and, second, that it demands minds producing ideas, occasionally possessed by inspired imaginations. Written compositions *must* to a greater or lesser degree reflect this, if students are to profit from written compositions in future vocations or professions. The writing skills that a student learns, practices, and masters during his high school English career are those that can be transferred to other academic disciplines, professions, or vocations. To repeat: writing is dependent upon ideas that in turn are responsible for everything that exists in the modern world.

But for any idea—from a topic for a ninth grade paragraph to a new commercial use for atomic energy—to be valid and then transformed into a workable instrument, it must be capable of passing at least a threefold test: First, is it presented in a logical order? Second, is the main idea closely related and carried through to each of its component parts? Third, is the idea sufficiently developed so that it is a complete presentation, without essentials being omitted or left to chance? These are three questions asked of any developing idea before its validity is accepted; in the composition program, they take the form of the three most important writing skills—organization, transition, and development.

Placing emphasis upon organization, transition, and development in the preparation of student themes is the most effective method by which the composition program can become meaningful to the student, as well as to improve his writing skill. For one reason, these areas are essential to both oral and written communications. In addition, they function as the basis on which the written composition communicates to the reader. Too many student-writers are totally ineffective in their compositions because they believe that to be vague is a sign of intelligence, and the reader will "know what I mean, anyway." Unfortunately, they are learning poor habits from various communications media that thrive upon their ability to avoid the specific and relegate the development of concrete details to mere matter-of-fact generalities. However, the high school composition program is not a training ground for rhetorical "windjammers"; continued emphasis upon these writing essentials—organization, transition, and development—must be maintained, or the writing program at the secondary level cannot carry out its primary objective of training disciplined writers who can effectively communicate a unified and fully developed idea.

2. The Guiding Purpose

Before a composition can be logically and effectively organized, the writer must first limit the area of his idea or topic. This can best be accomplished through a simple technique entitled the "Guiding Purpose." Defined as a "blanket" statement or a declarative sentence summary of the entire theme, the Guiding Purpose declares the intention of the composition. To be effective for the writer—since he is the one who receives the most benefit from the Purpose—this one or two sentence statement should contain several key words, preferably underscored for easy identification, that will control the theme and restrain the writer from extending beyond his intentions. Here is one example of a Guiding Purpose taken from a theme written during the sophomore year, and in which the writer's topic dealt with an experience from his summer vacation:

> *I* am *sincere* when I say that I was *homesick* for my *family* during that *first week* at *Camp Ken-Mont*.

Reduced to five areas of specific meaning, the above sentence indicates (1) that the completed theme will be written from the first person point of view (*I*); (2) that the writer's attitude toward his subject is one of sincerity; (3) the key idea of the entire theme, which is also the object of his sincerity, is his homesickness; (4) the general feeling of homesickness is made specific through the inclusion of the word "family," which is the real object of the writer's attitude; and (5) "first week at Camp Ken-Mont" specifically limits the time during which the entire experience occurred. If followed closely, this Guiding Purpose will assure the writer of a unified composition that will be free of needless digression. He will provide only those details that are necessary to his intentions.

3. The Theme Plan

The actual organization still finds the composition in the planning stage. This phase of the entire writing procedure is centered on the theme plan, a combination of the Guiding Purpose discussed in the preceding sub-section and a technique of organization that has been traditionally referred to as the outline. But whether it is labeled "plan" or "outline," this time honored device is still an effective weapon for maintaining logical arrangement throughout the entire theme. There are teachers who doubt the necessity for the plan in connection with the personal narrative theme, arguing that the order of a personal narrative or experience is automatic; events will assemble into proper chronological arrangement as the experience unfolds. They would rather wait to introduce the theme plan until students begin to write expository compositions, where the writer *must* select the most effective arrangement by which to present the details. There is nothing seriously wrong with this attitude, but if the student-writer learns to plan *all* of his themes well, then he will become instinctively aware of the necessity for organizing each and every idea that will eventually take the form of a written composition.

Like everything else in the composition program, outlining or planning must have a definite purpose—in this case it is to be employed in strict connection to the planning of written themes. Too often this device is nothing but time consuming with no other aim than to keep the students occupied during a given class hour (usually when the teacher is unprepared). If adopted toward this end—such as having the students outline a chapter from the textbook—the teaching of organization through the use of the theme plan becomes as sterile as isolated grammar. The true purpose of teaching the essentials of organization and the outlines that accompany them is to emphasize to students that before any writing can be attempted, the ideas of the composition should be first arranged in logical order, after which the concrete details in support of these ideas are to be included.

The theme plan also provides the teacher with the opportunity to see the young writer at work—the outline, when submitted with the completed composition, is the preparation; the theme is the finished product. This sensitive area of planning is unfortunately where too many students fail; they know what they want to say, but have difficulty in arriving at the best possible arrangement for their ideas. Assisting a student-writer to improve his *preparation* is often the key to improving his actual writing skill. When teaching the theme plan, it is really not essential to consume considerable time in the presentation of the various outline formats. The important objective is that some sort of plan is in evidence; whether or not it contains Roman numerals, capital letters, or Arabic numbers is inconsequential.

4. Transition

Transition is an area that concerns both the planning stage and the actual writing of the theme itself. Next to the problem of arranging ideas in their proper order, student-writers experience their greatest difficulty in transporting thoughts from one sentence, paragraph, or section of a theme to the one immediately following. This is really a simple matter, yet large numbers of college freshmen find this to be completely beyond their understanding because they were never before enlightened on such devices as the pronoun for transition, *careful* repetition of words or complete thoughts for transition, the synonym as a more subtle transitional technique, or some common words and phrases that will go far in making the transition from one area of the theme to another. For example, the table that follows, if placed in the hands of any writer from ninth to twelfth grades, can solve the problem of transition without wasting much classroom discussion:

Table of Transitional Words and Expressions

1. Demonstrative Pronouns: this
   that
   these
   those
2. Numerals and Synonyms for Numerals (used to imply a series): first
   in the first place
   to begin with
   second
   in the second place
   lastly
3. "And" and Its Synonyms (used to continue the same line of thought): again
   also
   in the next place
   once more

furthermore
moreover
likewise
besides
similarly
for example
for instance
in fact
4. "But" and Its Synonyms (to introduce opposed or contrasting thoughts):
 then
 nevertheless
 still
 however
 at the same time
 yet
 in spite of that
 on the other hand
 on the contrary
5. Degrees of Certainty: certainly
 surely
 doubtless
 indeed
 perhaps
 possibly
 probably
 anyhow
 anyway
 in all probability
 in all likelihood
 in any case
6. Consequence or Result: therefore
 consequently
 accordingly
 hence
 then
 thus
 as a result
 in consequence of this
 as might be expected
 so

If the traditional rules of English grammar can succeed in

convincing a student that a *transitive* verb passes over to or expresses action directed upon an object (the direct object), then surely the above table and the simple dictionary definition of *transition*—"passage from one place, state, stage of development or type to another"—can be equally successful in helping him to remember that the reader of his composition must be transported from one thought to the other without being forced to endure confusing time, place, or action gaps. For example, when the reader receives in the body of a composition specific details in support of the generalizations presented in the introduction, he is placed in the same position as "Jack's clenched fist," which is transported onto the nose of "John" by the transitive verb "hit." In other words, student-writers must be made to realize that transition is the key to a unified theme; the alert writer never isolates a single topic from the main idea of the entire composition.

5. Development

The last of the three essential writing skills to be considered is development and its application to the single paragraph. Too often student-writers are under the impression that a paragraph is merely equivalent to any number of words—from five to five hundred—and is distinguishable by the one-inch marginal indentation of the first word. The teacher who announces a theme assignment that is to be completed within the limits of a three or four paragraph development is almost immediately confronted with inquiries concerning length. When beginning composition students display more concern for filling a certain number of pages with their youthful scrawls than with the proper knowledge of what exactly constitutes a complete theme, the time has come for the entire class to be exposed to the proper definition of the paragraph. Out of necessity, this must be done as quickly as possible, for the student-writer cannot fulfill the aims of his Guiding Purpose until he has thoroughly mastered the areas of paragraph and theme development.

The traditional definition of a paragraph being a group of sentences that expresses a complete thought is a poor one because it is too general. Instead, student-writers should be shown the relationship of paragraph to the entire theme; like the entire theme of which it is a component, the paragraph has three parts; introduction (only now the term changes to "topic sentence"), body, and conclusion. Its length is never measured in terms of the number of words, but rather by the number of *details* needed to carry out the aim of the topic sentence, the key to any paragraph. Like the Guiding Purpose that was discussed in connection with the theme plan, the topic sentence controls; only in this case the area of control is limited to merely a *part* of the entire composition. The sentence must contain certain key words that will hold the paragraph to one specific thought, and the paragraph is never completed or fully developed until there is a sufficient number of details to support these words. As an example, a major paragraph division from the Guiding Purpose in Subsection 2 (page 35) that reads "*I am sincere* when I say that I was *homesick* for my *family* during that *first week* at *Camp Ken-Mont*" might be introduced by the following topic sentence:

> Until this summer, I have never been separated from Mike, my older brother, and I could not possibly see how the five boys with whom I shared a cabin would be able to take his place.

The direct relationship of topic sentence to Guiding Purpose is made clear when the student-writer can see that "Mike, my older brother" is one area of the larger "family," and "the five boys with whom I shared a cabin" is a part of "that first week at Camp Ken-Mont." Also, the attitude of the writer when he states that he could not possibly see how these five boys could take Mike's place is one aspect of his overall homesickness. Now in the same manner by which the topic sentence took its roots from the Guiding Purpose, the deails that will form the main body of this paragraph will have their origin from the key ideas of the topic sentence: namely, the close relationship with Mike during past summers and the description and activities of the five boys who are not able to eradicate the writer's desire to return to that relationship. It is for this reason—or, more accurately, it constitutes one of the reasons—that the writer was homesick for his family during that first week at Camp Ken-Mont.

When the supporting details that will substantiate this reason are complete, then the paragraph will be sufficiently developed; when the theme contains sufficient paragraph units to complete the intentions of the Guiding Purpose, then it too will be fully developed. The length of the completed composition, then, will depend upon the writer's ability to furnish enough concrete details to support the topic sentence of each paragraph, and the implication of the term "support"—whether it is applied to personal narrative, descriptive, or expository writing—is that the writer supplies no more nor no less than the key words have indicated. In this manner, when the Guiding Purpose of the theme and the topic sentence of the paragraph are strictly adhered to, the finished composition—because it has employed the basic essentials of organization, transition, and development—will be easily and quickly assimilated by the reader.

6. The Importance of Teaching Organization, Transition, and Development

The importance of teaching the techniques of organization, transition, and development is made perfectly clear after the first set of themes has been submitted. Now the composition teacher discovers the profound respect his students have for his position and knowledge. In fact this tribute will be so great that his student-writers will even acknowledge his ability to read their minds. For somewhere during their brief exposures to academic training, too many high school students have become obsessed with the idea that adults need only partial information in order to gain a thorough understanding of what teenagers are attempting to communicate to them. As a result, oral communication to parents and friends and written communication to English teachers is devoid of concrete material or utterly deficient in information necessary to complete the meaning of a clearly unified idea.

One of the composition teacher's most important tasks, therefore, is to impress upon his class the realization that the reader of a theme can only understand the material that actually appears on the paper, and thoughts that were omitted with the attitude of "You know what I mean!" have no way of being understood. Close attention to the three essential areas discussed in this section is an effective method by which student-writers can be exposed to the necessity for *complete* communication of a single idea. But this is often neglected by teachers of English because it takes time and patience, both in the classroom and during the lengthy hours of theme reading, before there is any evidence of positive results. However, the training of young students in the basic skills of writing disciplined prose was never intended for the glamorous or entertaining qualities of modern education. The complete development of ideas, along with their organization and transition, can only be mastered through constant writing practice.

Section V

TOPICS FOR STUDENT THEMES

1. The Teacher's Responsibility
2. The Results of Inexperience
3. What Constitutes a Legitimate Writing Assignment?
4. The Need to "Know Your Students"
5. Specific Topics for Student Themes
6. More Formal Writing Projects

1. The Teacher's Responsibility

As in any skill, the teaching of composition at the high school level is a coöperative effort on the part of both students and teachers. The student-writer who succeeds in deriving the maximum benefit from constant writing practice is the one who will conscientiously seek to advance the quality of his prose from one theme to the next. He does this by applying the corrections and recommendations which his instructor has noted on last week's theme to the next immediate writing assignment and by voluntarily attempting additional writing practice beyond the number of compositions required for the course. On the other hand, the composition teacher who is successful in bringing to the surface the full writing potentials of his students does so because he has not only provided them with ample opportunity for developing and practicing their writing skills, but he has also offered valuable assistance in suggesting material or furnishing specific topics for themes. Through his having experienced both adolescence and adulthood, the composition teacher can set before his student-writers a wealth of suggestive and didactic ideas from which they can select parallels that will coincide with their own spheres of experience. There is never any doubt about his students *wanting* to write or being aware of the importance for doing so in a disciplined and correct manner, for he matches their desires with his eagerness to share in their experiences.

The teacher's awareness that his student-writers realize the pleasures gained from clear communication and can understand its values and rewards to their futures, plus the knowledge that they will derive the benefits of constructive criticism from a conscientious and competent reader, will serve to augment the contribution of the composition program to the overall secondary curriculum. Yet unless the teacher can direct the complex but important facets of teenage life into the pages of his students' writing, he will quickly discover that the development of their writing skill is being hampered to a great extent as the result of his own erudite stubbornness. Perhaps the largest single reason behind the failure of any composition program is the damnable insistence of too many teachers that their students attempt nothing but scholarly trivia on literary criticism, an exercise that is beyond the reach of even their own meager capabilities.

2. The Results of Inexperience

In order for the composition program to serve effectively as a training ground for the improvement of student writing, the teacher must always remember that his duty is not to prepare his students for careers as professional writers, but to train them to communicate a single or a series of unified ideas in a disciplined prose style. Too often youngsters enrolled in high school English classes are forced to expound on topics that are completely beyond their levels of understanding or familiarity. Here, for example, is a "discriminate" selection of theme topics (actually assigned by high school English teachers) by grades, all of which are guaranteed to produce nothing but mental suffering on the part of students who must attempt to develop ideas from them and teachers who must read the finished products:

GRADE NINE:
1. Select a character from *Ivanhoe* to illustrate Sir Walter Scott's keen sense of the past.
2. Develop the idea of the sea as a primary cause of the desolation of Odysseus.

GRADE TEN:
1. *Julius Caesar* has been called the first of Shakespeare's

maturer tragedies. Do you agree that it is mature? Why or why not?
2. Illustrate and support with concrete examples how Shakespeare, through variation in rhythm, stress, pause, and tone, conveys the moods of the main characters in *As You Like It*.

GRADE ELEVEN:
1. In what poem does Edgar Allan Poe most fully develop the idea that "Poetry is the rhythmic creation of beauty?"
2. What is the role of the Mississippi River in Mark Twain's *The Adventures of Huckleberry Finn*?

GRADE TWELVE:
1. Substantiate a common criticism of Dylan Thomas: that his imagination could transport him anywhere, but whereever it takes him, he sees nothing but himself.
2. How is Prufrock's fear of ordinary living measured by his own standards?

As can be readily seen, these are not topics for high school students; rather, they are essay examination questions or term paper assignments for either undergraduate or graduate courses in literature. They are the result of the inexperienced teacher who is determined, regardless of the consequences, to make use of his "intensified concentration" in English or American literature.

The beginning teacher, schooled only in the study of literature and literary criticism before he is turned loose upon the high school composition program, is too often unable to make the transition from the college lecture hall-seminar room atmosphere to that of the secondary English classroom; therefore, the theme topics that he assigns to his students closely resemble those of his own upper division English courses. The outcome of this teacher's lack of education in teaching composition at the high school level will take the form of poorly constructed themes—lacking in effectiveness of communication and presentation of logical material—from students who are groping for ideas and struggling to fit them into the realm of their limited comprehension of the assigned topics. This is not to infer that literature has no place in the high school composition program, but only to suggest emphatically that before any topic can be justified as a theme assignment it must be within the limits of the high school student writer's experience and understanding.

3. What Constitutes a Legitimate Writing Assignment

Reduced to the simplest of terms, the high school English teacher can expect the best possible results from his students' compositions the moment that he chooses to climb down from his literary ivory tower and realize two elementary facts: (1) that between the ages of fourteen and eighteen, his students are living amidst a world of rich, varied experience which affect them daily and (2) they are yearning to communicate these experiences to someone of the adult society—preferably to a "someone" who is not a member of their immediate family. Since these opportunities for teenagers to communicate on a level that is above the late afternoon or evening "bull sessions" are limited, the composition program provides a natural outlet for written records of real and meaningful events. No matter what the area of the general assigned topic, if the student is at all familiar with it, he will be able to communicate a sustained idea that reflects upon his own experience. This will not only result in themes that are "alive" with the student's attitude toward a specific subject, but it will provide the essential motivation so necessary for the success of the composition program. The student will *want* to write when he is made to understand that *what* he has to say is just as important as the way in which he states it.

However, a word of warning might be in order at this point, lest the beginning composition teacher becomes the unhappy victim of his own eager benevolence. The high school composition program cannot function without strict but logical discipline. To allow students *carte blanche* in the selection of theme topics or the methods by which these topics are to be developed is to defeat the purpose of advancing their writing skill to a point where they will be able to attain proficiency in several areas of written communication. Therefore, the composition teacher must assume the responsibility for controlling the subject matter and methods of theme development, while at the same time remain alert to the interests, motivations and abilities of his students. In direct reference to theme topics, the more the teacher knows about his students the more the task of conceiving ideas and composing topics for their compositions becomes easier; for him concurrently, the themes themselves will increase in quality.

4. The Need to "Know Your Students"

Becoming *fully* acquainted with the likes, dislikes, and interests of between 120 and 150 students is too much to ask of any teacher during a nine month period. For one reason, individual conferences or interviews, perhaps the only opportunity for student and teacher to become really familiar with each other, would carry too far into the term to accomplish their purpose of discovering the range of the student's experiences and utilizing these experiences in his themes. The only alternative that the conscientious composition teacher has for acquiring some familiarization with his student-writers is a poor second to the personal interview, yet it must suffice until the advent of better teaching conditions and opportunities. Therefore, at the beginning of each term, each student should be required to complete a form somewhat similar to the one below; this completed form would then be retained on file and perhaps even passed on from one teacher to the next:

Name_____Age_____Grade_____
Father's Occupation_____
How many brothers and/or sisters?—————Ages:———
—————
—————
—————

List the subjects that interest you the most:

List the extra-curricular activities in which you participate:

List any hobbies that you have:

What do you plan to do after graduation from high school?

What are your plans for an eventual career?

How do you spend most of your spare time during the week?

What do you do during the week-ends?

Where do you usually spend your summers, and what do you do there?

List some of the more interesting places that you have visited:

What types of books do you enjoy the most?

List five (5) books that have impressed you the most, and briefly state your reasons: _____

If you have a part-time job, either during the school year or the summer, state your position, principal duties, and employer:

List five (5) to ten (10) possible theme topics about which you would be interested in writing during this term: _____

After these questionnaires have been completed and returned, the teacher will quickly discover that even though he has as many as 150 students, their areas of interest insofar as possible subject matter for themes is concerned will be generally similar. Therefore, it will not be necessary to compile a separate list of topics for each student. The value of such a form at the beginning of the term is that it provides the teacher with some familiarity with his students; if he is aware of their likes and dislikes, immediate interests and tentative plans for the future, then he can better formulate the theme topics toward the area of the writers' own experiences. The result will be concrete themes from student-writers who are *familiar* with the subjects of their themes, not clumsy attempts at abstract literary criticism about which they are not even qualified to write.

5. Specific Topics for Student Themes

The following list of theme topics is closer to what the composition teacher might demand from his students:

1. When I am introduced to a stranger, I look him over carefully and derive a first impression.
2. I believe that trustworthiness is the most important quality of friendship.
3. Arkansas is an ideal location for an industrial site.
4. The South is greatly in need of industrial development.
5. I fail to understand why men have always been considered superior to women.
6. I shall select an occupation that holds for me a great deal of respect and honor, in addition to a large income.
7. The athletic coach works hard with boys who are not completely developed physically and who have little knowledge of the sport in which they are engaged.
8. The athletic coach is a dedicated man because he devotes himself to the benefits of others instead of his own gain.
9. In order to halt monopolies, the Federal government has adopted laws to make such business illegal.
10. A monopoly newspaper is one that has complete control of an area of distribution.
11. Albert Schwcitzer is my example of a legendary hero.
12. The popularity of basketball is steadily increasing.
13. I consider the word *love* to be the most important in any language.
14. Whether or not to advance his education and the type of institution of higher learning to attend are major considerations of the high school senior.
15. The high school graduate must decide which is the best for him—the large university or the small college.
16. I believe that hero worship is a sign of immaturity.
17. Most teenagers have heroes for whom they have tremendous respect.

18. Parents must plan for the future of their children.
19. The purpose of William L. Shirer's biography of Adolf Hitler is to present the fanatical genius to the world in order to show how criminally insane he actually was.
20. *Mutiny on the Bounty* appealed directly to my longing for adventure.
21. Every year, automobile manufacturers increase the horsepower of their products.
22. Social clubs are an important part of a high school student's life.
23. I have my own idea of the qualities a girl should have.
24. It is important to make a good impression on the first date.
25. A crisis in an individual's life arises with every birthday, and the sixteenth is no more crucial than any other.
26. Everyone enjoys luxuries, although the most common are not recognized as such.
27. I recognized several members of my own class after I read the realistic characterizations in Rudyard Kipling's *Soldiers Three*.
28. The football coach is a unique member of the high school faculty, for he possesses certain qualities not found in his more academic associates.
29. If wisely chosen, words may have the power to influence great numbers of people.
30. If I were to venture into the unknown area of space travel, I would worry more about the psychological problems than the physical.
31. A great many decisions concerning America's defense problems must come from the Pentagon in Washington.
32. War can be prevented if the warning signs are quickly discovered.
33. The childhood impression of Hell is an unhealthy picture of fire, brimstone, and devils garbed in scarlet cloaks.
34. Many prominent historical figures have wanted some great moment to remind the world of their greatness.
35. Once I have become addicted to a certain habit or way or life, I do not want to lose it and will go to great lengths to retain it.
36. There will always be men who constantly fight and claw their way to the top.

37. Each generation has produced a few great men who have been sensitive to everything around them.
38. Although *Gulliver's Travels* is a unique work, I have formed several opinions as to why it has been treasured for so long.
39. Writing compositions is no different from any other form of literature; there are standards that must be met before the writer can become successful.
40. My dreams seem to bear miracles from the dark and deep of the night.
41. I realize that I cannot live a fulfilling life without encountering hardships, decisions, and treachery.
42. I recently dreamed of a magnificent place, a land of beauty and cruelty.
43. I believe that the first seventeen years of my life have been rather unusual.
44. One beautiful summer day I lay on a hill by the sea, away from everyone.
45. I have always been taught to believe that death represents not only the end of life, but also the beginning of something better.

These suggested topics represent vast areas of a high school student's experience, but more accurately they are samples from three phases of his contact with people, places, and events around him: (1) direct encounter with a particular experience, (2) information gathered from the different academic disciplines that comprise his education, and (3) personal opinions based upon the influence of others' ideas. Also, the topics are general enough so that they can be easily revised when the teacher believes that the substitution of a key word or two will allow the student to adjust the subject to fit his own particular situation. Yet before this list of topics can be hurriedly accepted or scornfully cast aside by any composition teacher, it must be clearly understood that very few collections of subjects for student themes are easily or readily transferable from one classroom or school district to another. Students' experiences and ideas are as heterogeneous as their talents, and the modern philosophy of applying a common denominator to everything in education will not succeed in the composition program. Here variety must continue to be the one great seasoning.

6. More Formal Writing Projects

While no one can dispute that learning to write for the sheer enjoyment of expression is one of the more aesthetic pleasures to be derived from a course in written communication, the composition program cannot ignore some of its purely professional obligations. Therefore, students should also be disciplined in applying their writing skills to topics where the material must be obtained from sources outside of their own immediate experiences. The specific reference is to writing projects that are preceded by formal research into specialized subject areas or problems. Training high school students in the methods and materials of research is absolutely necessary, since higher education, professions, and even vocations will often require writing of a more formal or academic nature. Here is where the teacher must temporarily halt the flow of so called "experience writing" and interject into the program such projects as the book review, literary evaluations, and research papers. But these forms of writing are not at all inappropriate if the teacher will only pause to explain carefully to his students the correct procedures in gathering, digesting, and finally applying outside material to their written compositions. Real concern arises whenever students are let loose in a library without the slightest notions of *what* they are to do or *how* they are to do it.

However, these more formal writing projects, when inserted into the composition program at the high school level, should always be subordinate to themes that deal with the students' own experiences. The reasons are obvious. In the first place, those who are preparing for higher education will discover that each department within a college or university has its own requirements—especially in format and style—for academic papers. The other reason is that those students who plan to enter vocations immediately following graduation from high school will discover the same degree and amount of inconsistency in the attitudes of businesses and industrial firms toward the preparation of technical reports. For these reasons, then, the high school composition program cannot afford to overindulge in areas that are in a constant state of flux. The primary purpose of the program is to train students in the *fundamentals* of writing disciplined prose; the specialized aspects of writing will take care of themselves when the time and the need arises, which it generally does after graduation.

If the composition program can provide the high school student with sufficient practice in writing clear, disciplined prose, then he will certainly have no difficulty in adapting to the idiosyncracies of college departments or business corporations. But the sooner he can be disciplined during this practice period, when the major portion of his writing will be devoted to communicating his *own* ideas and experiences, the better will be his opportunity to succeed in writing what others demand. In the mind of the high school student, the desire to write is equally important as the writing itself. The teacher can stimulate this desire by providing theme topics that are closely related to the students' experiences. The resultant flame might not always glow "hard and gem-like," but it will assuredly produce a clear, eager, and steady beacon of communication.

Section VI

READING THE THEME

1. The Reading Process
2. A Sample Theme to Illustrate the Reading Process
3. Stage 1: The Guiding Purpose
4. Stage 2: The Outline
5. Stage 3: The First Reading
6. Stage 4: The Second Reading
7. Stage 5: The Third Reading
8. Stage 6: The Fourth Reading
9. Stage 7: The Final Evaluation

1. The Reading Process

The often quoted statement about anything worth doing is worth doing correctly is a basic tenet to reading student themes. To the inexperienced, the procedures that will be outlined in this section may seem exceedingly and outrageously lengthy, and the novice teacher might wonder if the reading of a single paper can possibly be accomplished within one or two hours. Yet the more themes that are read, the easier the process becomes, especially when the teacher begins to develop an awareness of the individual student's writing habits. Knowledge of the student-writer's personal qualities is especially important in a program that deals with highly subjective material, and the teacher must quickly realize that behind every sentence there is a highly sensitive imagination anxious to get special attention to the ideas presented in each theme. Of course there are areas of the composition that can be treated from a fairly objective point of view—and the reference here is obviously toward problems of spelling, grammar, punctuation, and mechanics. But the important point to remember is that even though the theme is comprised of several areas, and even if some of these areas are purely subjective and others strictly objective, the final evaluation must be based upon the function of the theme as a *single* entity in which *one* idea is to be effectively communicated to the reader.

To begin, the *ideal* process for reading a theme involves a review of seven major stages, which are really the principal areas of any written composition. These include (1) examining the Guiding Purpose to see that the writer has a compact but specific sentence summary; (2) reading the outline in order to evaluate the writer's planned presentation of his material; (3) a complete reading of the theme to see if the writer has followed his Guiding Purpose and outline; (4) a second reading of the theme solely for the purpose of judging its content; (5) a third reading of the theme in order to evaluate its organization, paragraph development, sentence and paragraph transition, and sentence and paragraph variety; (6) a fourth reading of the theme to check accuracy in spelling, grammar, punctuation, and mechanics; and (7) a final reading for the purpose of an overall evaluation in which the theme is given a grade and the teacher writes a brief critical comment of its good and poor qualities.

It will be readily discerned that the above procedure is extremely detailed, perhaps even unnecessarily so. However, this process is directed to the beginning teacher of composition who, until he gains sufficient experience in reading student themes, will find it best to devote more time to the reading of his theme assignments for two logical reasons. First, since the majority of beginning English teachers have had little or no experience in reading and evaluating themes, they must learn this craft quickly; therefore, the theme reading process must serve as a thorough on-the-job training program. Second, and this is true for the experienced teacher as well as the inexperienced, careful reading and evaluation of student themes is a scrupulous teaching process; since students write compositions for the purpose of learning how to improve their writing skills, the corrected theme is an essential lesson, and it must be carefully and diligently prepared as such.

After a time, as the teacher begins to "know" his student-writers, the separate stages of theme reading outlined above can be limited to perhaps three or four, thus reducing the number of hours necessary for correcting a theme assignment. Another short-cut—one that is both practical and profitable—can be achieved if the students are aware of the teacher's methods of reading their themes. In this way they will be able to apply the same process before the papers are submitted to the teacher, which is excellent training for sharpening their own abilities as critics. After all, one of the most important skills to be developed by any writer is the competence to see and correct his own mistakes before someone else does. The written composition can never be considered on a par with an examination; the student should be provided with all of the answers before he applies the problems to practical use.

2. A Sample Theme to Illustrate the Reading Process

To illustrate in greater detail the suggested procedure for reading and evaluating a composition, it might be well to demonstrate visually the seven stages presented in Subsection 1. Therefore, let the following narrative theme (transcribed here in the original), complete with Guiding Purpose and outline, serve as a sample:

He's Gone

GUIDING PURPOSE: My purpose is to tell about my dog and what happened to him.

I. First acquaintance
   A. White puppy
   B. Attraction to me
   C. Puppy pranks

II. Our good times together
   A. Pulling my sled
   B. Chasing rabbits
   C. Like one of the family
      1. Eating food
      2. "Skipper" Jones

III. "Skipper's" departure
   A. I had gone to school
   B. The real truth

Skipper was all mine, I guess he was the first thing that I really claimed as my own. He was just a white, cur dog, but he was a champion to me. I recieved him on my fourth birthday. He was cute like all pups and he took to me right off. I'm afraid my parents were a little doubtful in their acceptance of him. This feeling wasn't unfounded for Skipper took up chewing on the furniture, jumping at the wash on the clothesline, and chasing chickens. I always forgave him for his mischievous deeds even if no one else did.

By the time Skipper became fully grown, we were inseperable pals. In the winter he would pull my sled like a huskie. That is if I could bribe him with enough dog bisquits. He was also the best livestock dog that I have ever seen. Of course, I was only six at the time but he could put any chicken, cow, or pig to flight at my command. Many times Skipper was scolded by my father for putting livestock to flight without my commands. Even if we did have a few disagreements, Skipper was just like one of the family. In fact his real name was Skipper Jones. Since he was a member of the family, he ate like one. He was particularly fond of jelly sandwiches but any food was usually accepted with delight.

The last time I saw Skipper was when I was in the third grade. One night as I jumped off the school-bus there was no Skipper there to greet me. I didn't miss him much untill supper when I asked my dad if he had seen Skipper. Dad said that he had opened one of the barnyard gates on Skipper and had rushed through it and started running up the road. That had been the last time he had seen him. I confidently predicted that Skipper would be back in the morning but he wasn't. He never came back. I worried about him for several weeks and then forgot about him and the good times we had had together. Only last year did I find out the truth about Skipper. He had gone mad and bitten a salesman. Dad was then forced to distroy him and told me the story about Skipper running away to protect my feelings. I am glad he did.

Now, in the following seven sub-sections, observe the stages of the theme correcting process as they are applied to the above sample composition.

3. Stage 1: Guiding Purpose

EXAMINE THE GUIDING PURPOSE TO SEE THAT THE WRITER HAS A COMPACT BUT SPECIFIC SEN-

TENCE SUMMARY: Obviously, the sentence in the preceding sample theme—"My purpose is to tell about my dog and what happened to him."—is far too general to allow the writer to establish the main areas of his composition. In the first place, the first six words—"My purpose is to tell about"—are a waste of time and effort, since *every* theme is bound to "Tell about" something. Therefore, the last two parts of this sentence—"my dog" and "what happened to him"—must bear the entire weight of the effectiveness of the Guiding Purpose; but, as was immediately observed, this is almost impossible because they lack concreteness. The writer's dog is in reality a white, cur puppy who answers to the name of Skipper, and there is no reason why this cannot reinforce the original description. In this way, the main topic of the composition becomes limited to one specific character.

Now a serious revision of the occasion, weakly stated as "what happened to him," must also be limited, if for no other reason than to inform the *writer* of the time limit for his theme. According to its outline, the theme deals with three major instances in the relationship between the writer and his dog: their initial acquaintance, the good times that they had together, and the events leading to the dog's departure. Since these are the major divisions of the theme, they should be stated in the purpose so that the writer can easily apply them to his plan.

Therefore, a more accurate and useful restatement of the Guiding Purpose would look something like this: "From the moment of our first meeting, Skipper and I experienced good times together, but our friendship was cut short by his sudden departure."

4. Stage 2: The Outline

READ THE OUTLINE IN ORDER TO EVALUATE HOW THE WRITER HAS PLANNED THE PRESENTATION OF HIS MATERIAL: The writer of this theme has chosen to develop his presentation from three major areas: first acquaintance, our good times together, and Skipper's departure. A review of the outline will disclose that the order of this presentation is logical and the first two major areas contain a sufficient number of supporting details. However, the last section of the theme—"Skipper's" departure—might be difficult to develop because its two supporting details—"I had gone to school" and "The real truth"—are vague and create a large transition gap. In addition, the statement that the writer had gone to school is really not important; he discovers Skipper's absence upon his *return*. Perhaps a revision of this final paragraph plan would read:

III. Skipper's departure
    A. His absence noted when I got off the school-bus
    B. Dad said he had run away
    C. I did not discover the truth until last year

5. Stage 3: The First Reading

A COMPLETE READING OF THE THEME TO SEE IF WRITER HAS FOLLOWED HIS PURPOSE AND OUTLINE: This stage is closely related to Stage 2, the exception being that the outline is now applied to the completed composition. In this theme, it is impossible to determine whether or not the writer actually has followed his Guiding Purpose, since the original sentence summary had to be completely revised (see Subsection 3) to be effective. Notice, however, how the main criticisms against the outline (see Subsection 4) will also apply in this stage. The first two paragraphs strictly adhere to divisions of the outline, while the final paragraph, because the plan was vague, contains a great deal more than seems to have been intended. Although any outline should be flexible to allow the writer to add and delete as he sees necessary, obviously the writer of this theme would have had an easier task constructing the concluding paragraph had he provided himself with a plan similar to the revision in Stage 2 (see Subsection 4). But, for at least two-thirds of the composition, the writer has followed his outline; therefore, in regard to this theme, Stages Two and Three could easily have been combined.

However, there are many student-writers whose lazy dispositions will lead them to divorce the outline from the theme, which results only in haphazard organization. And until they can be prompted into a conscientious development of a theme plan before they begin to write the composition itself, this stage will have to be included separately in the theme reading process.

6. Stage 4: The Second Reading

A SECOND READING OF THE THEME SOLELY FOR THE PURPOSE OF JUDGING ITS CONTENT: The content, or the extent to which the writer develops his main idea, is primarily determined by the Guiding Purpose. Before a reader can accurately judge any piece of writing, he should have some idea of the writer's intentions. In this manner, purpose and content have a direct connection. If the original purpose of the theme under discussion—"My purpose is to tell about my dog and what happened to him."—were to be accepted without revision, then the content of the completed composition would have to be judged strictly on the basis of *everything* that had or has happened to "Skipper." Obviously, the theme does not fulfill the requirements of its original purpose. However, the suggested revision of the Guiding Purpose—From the moment of our first meeting, Skipper and I experienced good times together, but our friendship was cut short by his sudden departure—provides the reader with a basis for judging the content of the theme because it limits the heretofore general subject to an area that can be handled within the confines of a three paragraph composition.

Now let's pay attention to a specific criticism of the actual content of this theme. Although the writer has presented an adequate account of the relationship between him and his dog, he might be more specific in two important areas in order that the concluding paragraph will have greater force as a so-called tragedy in the life of a young boy. First, there is justification for a more detailed physical description of "Skipper." The only information as to this dog's appearance are "white, cur dog" and "cute" in the first paragraph. The more detail that can be presented concerning the main "character" of this narrative, the more the reader can understand the effect of "Skipper's" departure at the conclusion. This, therefore, provides meaning to the entire composition, and it also enables the writer to exhibit an emotional attitude toward his subject. Second, and also a point that parallels the first criticism, the writer has devoted too much material to "Skipper," which has the effect of excluding himself from the narrative. This results in a lack of emotional force at the conclusion of the composition, for the close attachment of a six-year-old boy to his dog has never really been developed.

What is essentially missing from this theme is the writer's *attitude toward his subject*, without which the narrative lacks individuality or identity—the experience could have happened to anyone. To prevent such a common occurrence as this in high school writing, the teacher must continue to emphasize the relationship of Guiding Purpose to content or material. If the student-writer can learn the value of stating his attitude in the purpose and then developing it in the composition, then his writing will lead directly to his *own* thoughts and experiences.

7. Stage 5: The Third Reading

A THIRD READING OF THE THEME IN ORDER TO EVALUATE ITS ORGANIZATION, PARAGRAPH DEVELOPMENT, SENTENCE AND PARAGRAPH TRANSITION, AND SENTENCE AND PARAGRAPH VARIETY: For the sake of clarity in presenting the discussion of this stage of the theme evaluation process, perhaps it might be wise to examine each subdivision separately.

A. ORGANIZATION: The order in which the writer of the sample theme presents his paragraph ideas is for the most part logical. The reason for this is that the order of presentation is dictated automatically by the events themselves. Here, then, can be observed one of the first "constants" of narrative writing: because the events almost always occur in rigid chronological order, the writer of a narrative theme need not be too concerned over which details to present first; improper placement of paragraph ideas will result in an arrangement so awkward that immediate detection is obvious. Therefore, the only possible arrangement for this theme is that which the writer employs—Skipper's arrival, his activities, and finally his departure. However, when applying this phase of Stage 5 to expository writing, the teacher will have to be careful to observe the order in which ideas are presented. The ultimate success of the expository theme depends heavily on the writer's ability to select an appropriate and logical order for the presentation of his material to the reader.

B. PARAGRAPH DEVELOPMENT: As explained in detail in Section IV, 5, paragraph development is based upon the writer's ability to furnish the reader with sufficient detail in order to support or substantiate the aims of the topic sentence. This is essential to the theme writing process because the reader is better able to discern the distinct divisions of the idea that the writer is attempting to communicate. In the sample theme, although the writer provides ample detail, it is difficult to determine the function of each paragraph simply because there is a decided lack of good topic sentences.

In the first paragraph, for example, there are *three* distinct ideas—(1) the writer as sole owner of Skipper, (2) a brief physical description of Skipper, and (3) the doubtful acceptance of Skipper by the writer's parents—all of which are weakly held together by the knowledge that Skipper is in the "pup" stage of his growth. By the second paragraph, the writer has become completely wedded to the idea of developing his paragraphs chronologically, a method that is certainly not the least distasteful. However, the paragraph also exists without benefit of a controlling topic sentence, and this time there are *two* separate ideas—(1) the close attachment of the writer to Skipper and (2) the latter's entrance into the immediate family circle. But in the final paragraph, the writer is at last able to control his idea under *one* definite topic sentence—the absence of Skipper at his usual place of greeting —and provide sufficient supporting details for the benefit of explaining to the reader *why* the particular situation existed. Therefore, the teacher can assume that even though the writer has done well in presenting a sufficient number of details for this narrative, he must—on the basis of the first two paragraphs—concentrate upon developing these ideas into complete paragraphs that are under the strict control of clear and well-defined topic sentences.

C. SENTENCE AND PARAGRAPH TRANSITION: For the most part, as in all pieces of narrative writing, the writer of the sample theme transports his sentence and paragraph ideas through to their conclusion on the vehicle of time. His external structural design is based upon the acquisition, growth, and departure of Skipper. Also, by focusing entire attention upon the dog, the writer is not faced with responsibility of dealing with several key areas of concentration. Therefore, and without much effort, almost all of the pronouns and transitional words and phrases have automatic reference to Skipper. The lapse in time or the confusions as to exact references that do occur in this composition are the result of poor sentence construction, not of any neglect in transition.

D. SENTENCE AND PARAGRAPH VARIETY: To detect a lack of sentence and paragraph variety in a composition is a simple matter, even at the very first reading. The monotony of this style-less paper will readily assert itself, and the teacher need only read it aloud to the writer in order to prove that the theme (and perhaps even the writer himself) is dull. If the student requires additional and more specific proof to understand this serious shortcoming, the teacher can compile a simple analysis of the theme in summary form. Something like the following, applied directly to the sample theme under discussion, can be readily assimilated by the student-writer:

Paragraph I: Sentence 1: Simple/Declarative
2: Complex/Declarative
3: Compound/Declarative
4: Simple/Declarative
5: Compound-Complex/Declarative

                         6: Complex/Declarative
                         7: Complex/Declarative
                         8: Complex/Declarative
                         Total: Simple: 2
                                Compound: 1
                                Complex: 4
                                Compound/Complex: 1
                                Declarative: 8
Paragraph II: Sentence 1: Complex/Declarative
                         2: Complex/Declarative
                         3: Complex/Declarative
                         4: Compound/Declarative
                         5: Simple/Declarative
                         6: Complex/Declarative
                         7: Simple/Declarative
                         8: Complex/Declarative
                         9: Compound/Declarative
                         Total: Simple: 2
                                Compound: 2
                                Complex: 5
                                Declarative: 9
Paragraph III: Sentence 1: Complex/Declarative
                          2: Complex/Declarative
                          3: Complex/Declarative
                          4: Complex/Declarative
                          5: Complex/Declarative
                          6: Compound-Complex/Declarative
                          7: Simple/Declarative
                          8: Complex/Declarative
                          9: Simple/Declarative
                         10: Simple/Declarative
                         11: Compound-Complex/Declarative
                         12: Simple/Declarative
                         Total: Simple: 4
                                Complex: 6
                                Compound/Complex: 2
                                Declarative: 12

Grand Total: Simple: 8
               Compound: 3
               Complex: 15
               Compound/Complex: 3
               Declarative: 29

From such an analysis as this, the student-writer can readily see why the teacher has labeled his theme as "dull" and lacking in variety: namely, that while it might be permissible for a news article in the local paper to be comprised of one-hundred percent declarative sentences, the writer of a personal narrative should attempt to communicate his own attitudes and emotions toward the subject about which he is writing. Although a theme can be grammatically and mechanically "perfect" (which this one certainly is not), it can still be a failing theme because the writer has not made it sufficiently appealing for someone to *want* to read it. What should be brought to this writer's attention, then, is that he can "attract" his reading audience through proper and discriminate use of interrogative, imperative, or exclamatory sentences.

To prepare a detailed summary like the one above for each and every theme is too much to ask of any teacher, no matter how conscientious he may be. However, here is one aspect of the theme reading process that can be accomplished in the classroom as part of a profitable lesson in self-criticism. If the teacher discovers that a sufficient number of student-writers is not paying strict attention to sentence and paragraph variety, he may wish to undertake a similar analysis with the entire class, selecting perhaps one of the more flagrant violators as a visual example. Then, he might select a theme in which the writer has practiced *good* use of variety and subject it to a similar analysis. Once the teacher believes that his students are aware of the importance of variety, he can require that each writer submit a summary of his sentences with the completed composition assignment. Just as in every other aspect of theme writing, the more responsibility that is placed upon the individual student for eliminating his own weaknesses, the quicker the errors will disappear.

8. Stage 6: The Fourth Reading

A FOURTH READING OF THE THEME TO CHECK ACCURACY IN SPELLING, GRAMMAR, PUNCTUATION, AND MECHANICS: Depending upon the abilities of his students, the composition teacher is likely to discover that this stage of the theme reading process is liable to consume a large portion of his time spent in reading a theme assignment—although it certainly should not! Yet, while this is far from the most important facet of the writing skill, it has a slight advantage over the other phases of theme writing because it is the most objective. Therefore, the composition teacher should investigate methods by which he can note errors of grammar, spelling, punctuation, and mechanics quickly, but plainly, so that they can be easily recognized by the student-writers. The most obvious means is the employment of a correction chart that is usually found in most composition texts. However, if the teacher should find himself without such an aid in his particular text, he can easily compose one of his own, complete with symbols and as elaborate as he chooses. The following chart, entitled "A Composition Grading and Check List," might serve as a useful illustration:

A Composition Grading and Checking List

CORRECTION SYMBOL	ERROR	EXAMPLE OF ERROR	CORRECTION OF ERROR
ROS	Run-on Sentence	I received an electric train that Christmas but I was too young to appreciate it.	I received an electric train that Christmas, but I was too young to appreciate it.
FRAG	Sentence Fragment	Jim can ask his dad for the money. Or get a job and earn it himself.	Jim can ask his dad for the money or get a job and earn it himself.
AWK	Awkward Sentence Structure	The spray is effective that it can control the disease with one gallon.	One gallon of this spray is all that is needed to control the disease.
SP	Spelling	dependant grammer fundimental embarass	depend*e*nt gramm*a*r fund*a*mental embar*r*ass

PAG	Error in Agreement of Pronoun with Antecedent	I am a member of the group *who* went to Washington in the spring.	I am a member of the group *that* went to Washington in the spring.
S-VAG	Error in Agreement of Verb with Subject	He *don't* know a thing about atomic submarines.	He *doesn't* know a thing about atomic submarines.
COMP	Faulty or Illogical Comparison	Jack can hit the ball as well as his brother.	Both Jack and his brother can hit the ball a great distance.
P-REF	Faulty or Loose Pronoun Reference	Their splendid uniforms enhanced the soldiers' appearance.	The soldiers' splendid uniforms enhanced their appearance.
MOD	Misplaced Modifier	His bayonet to the front of his rifle was attached.	His bayonet was attached to the front of his rifle.
OM	Omission of Needed Word(s)	The team is much stronger this season than 1960.	The team is much stronger this season than *it was in* 1960.
SI	Split Infinitive	We had *to quickly change* for our first number.	We had *to change* quickly for our first number.
ST	Shift in Verb Tense	Finks *faded* back a few yards and *throws* a fifty-yard pass.	Finks *faded* back a few yards and *threw* a fifty-yard pass.
P	Error in Punctuation	He observed the blue sky, and the dark green of the still grass.	He observed the blue sky and the dark green of the still grass.
CASE	Case Error (to include the omission of the apostrophe)	Give that to *who*ever you want. That was my parents last wish.	Give that to *whom*ever you want. That was my parents' last wish.
RED	Redundancy and Wordiness	He thrust his pointed sword into the proud, breathing breast of	He stabbed Titus. or He killed Titus by

		Titus and saw the red blood issue forth to proclaim his death.	stabbing him through the heart.
REP	Unnecessary Repetition	Why was *he* a good player? *He could* hit, *he could* run, and *he could* throw.	He was a good player because he could hit, run, and throw.

The lengths to which such a correction chart can be extended are almost limitless; the sample above has been condensed for the sake of brevity. For instance, in place of the lone "P" to indicate all errors of punctuation—comma, semicolon, period, quotation marks, apostrophe—the teacher can insert a symbol for each area; also, he can certainly add other areas not mentioned in this chart—a symbol for capitalization is a necessity. The advantage of the teacher composing his own chart is that—as far as correction symbols are concerned—it is more categorized and varied than the one that may be found in the textbook; additions and deletions can be easily made to fit the needs of a particular class of student-writers, since the majority of competent composition teachers tend to shy away from presenting students with examples of errors which they have not yet made or have completely eliminated from their themes.

However, one point must never be forgotten: a correction chart of this sort is only effective as long as the students are completely familiar with the grammatical and mechanical points that it covers. It must be composed and distributed at the very beginning of the term and thoroughly explained before it becomes operational. Once this had been accompplished, then it can be an efficient aid to the teacher as well as a learning device for his students. Observe, therefore, the application of the correction chart to the sample theme of this section:

He's Gone

ROS:
Comma splice

Skipper was all mine, I guess he was the first thing that I really claimed as my own. He was just a white, cur dog, but he was a champion to me. I recieved him on my fourth birthday. He was cute like all pups and he took to me right off. I'm afraid my parents were a little doubtful in their acceptance of him. This feeling wasn't unfounded for Skipper took up chewing on the furniture, jumping at the wash on the clothesline, and chasing chickens. I always forgave him for his mischievous deeds even if no one else did.

By the time Skipper became fully grown, we were inseperable. In the winter he would pull my sled like a huskie. That is if I could bribe him with enough dog bisquits. He was also the best livestock dog that I have ever seen. Of course, I was only six at the time but he could put any chicken, cow, or pig to flight at my command. Many times Skipper was scolded by my father for putting livestock to flight without my commands. Even if we did have a few disagreements, Skipper was just like one of the family. In fact, his real name was Skipper Jones. Since he was a member of the family, he ate like one. He was particularly fond of jelly sandwiches but any food was usually accepted with delight.

The last time I saw Skipper was when I was in the third grade. One night as I jumped off the school bus there was no Skipper there to greet me. I didn't miss him much untill supper when I

ROS: , between two independent clauses

ROS: , between two independent clauses

P: , to set off subordinate element from main clause

SP

AWK: Not really. Be accurate—you jumped *from* the bus or *hurriedly ran down the steps of the bus.*

RED: Where? Since actual location is not really important, why not substitute ". . . *waiting* to greet me"?

SP

SP
RED: inaccurate; try "accepted me immediately
RED: inaccurate; *began* to chew . . . jump . . . chase

SP—also capitalized
FRAG

ROS: , between two independent clauses

ROS: , between independent clauses

AWK: impossible, unless the gates fell on Skipper (which

READING THE THEME

OM: who—
your father or
Skipper?

ROS: , between
independent
clauses

REP: not
necessary the
second time.
The relationship between
"good times"
and Skipper has
already been
established.

asked my dad if he had seen Skipper. Dad said that he had opened the barnyard gates on Skipper and had rushed through it started running up the road. That had been the last time he had seen him. I confidently predicted that Skipper would be back in the morning but he wasn't. He never came back. I worried about him for several weeks and then forgot about him and the good times we had. Only last year did I find out the truth about Skipper. He had gone mad and bitten a salesman. Dad was then forced to distroy him and told me the story about Skipper running away to protect my feelings. I am glad he did.

apparently they
did not)
OM: You need
a conjunction
here

OM: Auxiliary
verb needed if
you want to
continue the
same tense

SP

MOD: Modifies
the verb "told";
this is not the
reason why
Skipper ran
away.

Obviously, then, the correction chart with its accompanying symbols can be a definite timesaver, especially if the teacher does not have to waste additional effort by including remarks concerning grammar, punctuation, and mechanics in his final criticism of the theme. Heavy but clear application of the traditional red pencil symbols in the margin, although under constant attack from progressive reformers, is still an effective method for shaking most student-writers from their lethargic and half-hearted proof-reading habits and illuminating the errors of their ways. The writer of the above theme is now in possession of clearly defined areas of his own weaknesses in sentence structure which he can easily correct before next week's theme assignment. Also, the teacher and he have composed a smaller version of a workbook; he has *his own* sentences to correct and revise after he has studied the appropriate principles.

9. Stage 7: The Final Evaluation

A FINAL READING FOR OVERALL EVALUATION—THE THEME IS GIVEN A GRADE AND WRITTEN CRITICISM, *BOTH* POSITIVE AND NEGATIVE: The final reading of any composition is perhaps the most important stage of the entire theme reading process. In the first place, a paper should never be dismissed immediately following the final mark of correction or criticism. Just as student-writers are apt to overlook several errors when they fail to proof-read their papers, teachers are likely to commit the same blunders if papers are read too hastily and without *thorough* evaluation. Therefore, teachers can use this stage as an opportunity to discover errors that they might have overlooked during a previous reading or to delete critical remarks that might have resulted from hasty misinterpretations or judgments. Second, during this final reading the teacher can view the composition in its complete perspective, a task that is absolutely essential before the final critical evaluation can be addressed to the writer.

The importance of this critical "message" from the teacher to the student-writer can never be over-emphasized, although it is too often underestimated. Actually, this is a summary of all remarks and symbols found in the margins of the paper, in addition to suggestions for improvement on the next theme assignment. But the criticism does not, of course, always have to be negative; if the paper is a good one, this should be mentioned, and the reasons for its quality clearly stated. Yet a teacher must never feel obligated to "find" positive points in a paper when none exist. A great injustice and rank indecency are committed when a student is informed that he has done something well when, in reality, he has performed poorly. If a theme fails to meet the standards of good, disciplined prose writing, the teacher is required according to the duties imposed on his noble profession to inform the writer of this and fully explain how the paper and the student's general writing ability can be improved. This is teaching; to do less is hypocrisy and professional dishonesty.

Section VII

REVISIONS AND RE-WRITINGS

Revisions and Rewriting

After the theme reading process has been completed, there remains yet another task before the obligations of a composition assignment can be met: the revising and rewriting of returned themes. The responsibility for this is almost entirely with the student-writer, and for this reason it has been omitted from Section VI. But, as in all phases of the composition program at the high school level, the revising of corrected themes must be closely supervised by the teacher.

The corrected theme must always be considered an important step toward the writing of the next theme assignment. The teacher reinforces this theory by a conscientious effort to read each theme thoroughly, criticize it, and then return it *promptly* to the writer. The writer, in turn, revises or rewrites the returned theme with the aim of eliminating his current errors from future compositions. To eliminate undue expenditures of time and paper, and to make students more conscious of their theme errors, the teacher may want to initiate a procedure whereby student-writers can keep a fairly detailed and up-to-date account of their writing deficiencies. The following "Theme Correction Chart" is helpful, especially to those teachers who collect and file corrected themes, because it remains in the student's possession for easy reference and immediate consultation:

Assignment #	Title	Grade	Original Version	ERRORS Corrected To Read:	Reason for Correction	Teacher's Comments
1	He's Gone	C	My purpose is to tell about my dog and what happened to him.	From the moment of our first meeting, Skipper and I experienced good times together, but our friendship was cut short by his sudden departure.	My purpose is too general; it does not clearly define the main areas of the topic, nor does it control and limit the theme to one complete and specific purpose.	Although you provide a good deal of information concerning your dog and his activities, you fail to convince the reader that Skipper really meant anything to you or that his loss affected you in some way. In other words, you fail to inject enough emotion into your sentences—and therefore your ideas and feelings.

You must also be aware of sentence variety; your theme is dull because you write only declarative sentences.

Finally, you must pay attention to correctness in your sentence structure. Consult your text and correction chart and study those principles of grammar, spelling, and punctuation that you have violated. |
| | | | Of course, I was only six at the time but he could put any chicken, cow, or pig to flight at my command. | Of course, I was only six at the time, but he could put any chicken, cow, or pig to flight at my command. | ROS: When two or more independent clauses are joined by a coordinating conjunction (and, but, or, nor, for), a comma (,) precedes the conjunction. | |

As with all of the other suggestions that have been set forth in this manual, the "Theme Correction Chart" can easily be expanded or simplified to meet the needs of a particular group of student-writers or the desires of the composition teacher. More than anything else, it is merely one of the many devices aimed at encouraging students to help themselves as much as possible toward improving their writing skills.

Likewise, the important task of reading and criticizing theme assignments is not to be considered a bothersome or inconvenient chore, but a direct aid to improving the quality of student writing. This is the only method by which students can be taught to write: by constant writing practice and thoughtful application of sound criticism of this practice. And because the majority of students in a composition class will dedicate themselves toward a conscientious effort to produce what they believe to be worthwhile themes, it is only fair that teachers should display a similar attitude through a willingness to read thoroughly what has been written. Perhaps the most serious detriment to the morale of the high school composition program is present in the form of disinterested teachers who fail to focus serious attention upon the reading of student themes; consequently, students become aware of this lack of interest, and their desires to achieve and perfect disciplined writing habits decline. But the teachers who work *with* their student-writers will observe the eventual success of the composition program—a student-teacher partnership built firmly upon coöperation, effort, and improvement.

Section VIII

SAMPLE THEMES FOR PRACTICE

1. A Note on the Sample Themes
2. Narrative
3. Exposition
4. The Book Review

1. A Note on the Sample Themes

Because the problems of theme reading are numerous and varied, and many readers undoubtedly sense the need for an opportunity to examine additional student themes more closely and without relying upon the pontifical "do's" and "don't's" found in Section VI, this section has been inserted into the manual for whatever benefit it may provide—both immediate and in the future. Therefore, the following sample themes (Subsections 2-4), each complete with a Guiding Purpose and outline, are presented for possible dissection and discussion by individuals or groups. These are random selections, transcribed here in the original, and no attempts have been made to alter the material or methods of presentation. The quality of this set ranges from poor to good, but in the final analysis the individual reader must determine the positive and negative points of each theme.

2. Narrative

#1
The Green Gander

Guiding Purpose: To show, by illustration, how my materialistic values changed as I grew older.
  I. My junior year in high school
      A. New car suggested for going downtown
      B. Would rather take the old one
      C. Junior high days recalled
          1. 1949 Studebaker—"Green Gander"
          2. My serious objections to it
  II. Reminiscence of day during junior high school
      A. Embarrassed to be seen in old car
      B. Argument for new car

1. My point of view
    a. Embarrassing for Dad
    b. Shopping hard for Mom
    c. Dating almost impossible for Bob
    d. No fresh air; broken doors
2. Dad's side
    a. Gets us where we want to go
    b. Good conversational piece
    c. NO NEW CAR!

III. Back to present
  A. Chugged toward business section
  B. Parked in grocery lot
  C. Woman stumbled over curb at sight of car
  D. Greeted her with "Good morning"

"Take the new car," Dad suggested when I asked him for the keys to go downtown.

"Oh, I think I'd rather take the 'Green Gander,' Dad," was my reply. "Somehow, I feel more comfortable with it."

He smiled and handed me the keys to the 1949 Studebaker, which we had christened "The Green Gander" twelve years before. Maybe he remembered, like I did, my objections to the old car during my junior high days. I recalled, with the trace of a smile, that day five years before when....

I could hear our old car rattling down the paved street toward the junior high school building where I waited impatiently for my father. As I walked toward the place where it would stop for me, I looked around to be sure nobody would see me get in the 1949 Studebaker. The car came grudgingly to a halt beside me. I gazed scornfully at the many rough spots and dents in the pitiful vehicle and walked around it to get in. I tried the door handle and then remembered that it did not open from the outside. Dad leaned over and opened it from the inside, and I climbed in beside him.

"How was school today, honey? He asked his usual question in his usual nonchalant manner.

And I answered in my usual I-couldn't-care-less spirit, "Fine, I guess."

The car jerked along, and we sat in silence. I was determined to let Dad know how I felt about our outmoded means of transportation, so I lightly said, "We're going to buy a new car soon, aren't we, Dad?"

"Huh?" It was the reply I had expected, so I slowly and deliberately repeated my question. "A new car? What would we do with a new car? This one gets us around just fine."

I wouldn't give up. I tried to appeal to his pride and sense of responsibility. "You can't imagine how silly you look, Dad —a Studebaker, no less! People must think you're straight from nowhere. And think of the rest of us! Mom has to take this old thing to the grocery store every week and fuss with doors that don't work. No wonder we never have any food; Mom hates to shop in the old thing! And Bob will be starting to date before long. I can just see him and some girl going to the Christmas Formal in this klunky thing! Nobody can have any fresh air because the windows will hardly roll down. And once you get them down, they won't roll back up without cracking. Oh—I forgot—there is one way to fresh air. It comes in through the holes under the gas pedal. Maybe it'd be a good thing if *both* doors didn't open from the outside. Then we could never get in again. We'd *have* to buy a new car." I finished with a flourish. My cheeks were red with the excitement of argument, and I sat forward in the seat, anxiously awaiting my father's reply.

But Dad wasn't to be taken in by my rationalization. He paused, sighed heavily, and began. "It doesn't matter to me what people think. You'd be surprised how handy this car can be at times. It's a better conversational piece than the weather." I winced at his dry humor. "We won't be getting a new car for quite awhile." His stern voice told me I had lost.

As the stop light flashed green, I returned to the present. I chugged my way toward the business section, smiling over the memories of my dislike for the "Green Gander." Parking in the grocery lot, I saw a woman stumble over the curb when she spotted the delapidated auto jump to a stop. I hopped out, after struggling with the door for a few minutes, and walked toward the entrance to the food store. I said "Good morning" to the confused woman who opened the door to her late model Lincoln.

#2
A Tornado

Guiding Purpose: My guiding purpose is to describe my experience of being in a tornado while I was on a golf course.

I. My previous attitude toward storms
   A. I never minded them
   B. They seemed to reveal God
II. The day was somewhat different than any other
   A. I was playing with Mike Johnson
   B. The weather was threatening to some extent
   C. The storm came
   D. We ran to the clubhouse
III. We observed the damages
   A. Damage was done to our physical possessions
   B. Damage was inflicted on our morale and confidence

I can recall a frightful storm last summer. Until this time, I never had any particular passion toward storms, but I didn't hate them either. Sometimes I even enjoyed them. It filled me with awe to watch the nervous lightening and to hear and to feel the wind blow through the screens into my face. The tornado was different. I didn't enjoy it.

Mike Johnson, a personal friend, and I were playing golf—the third hole of Rolling Acres Golf Course. We noticed the unusual color of the sky, but when we played golf, we never let a bit of threatening weather interfere. Instead, we usually played much faster to show God that we are strong men. By the time we got to the third green, however, God had begun to release the clutch of his storm's machine. A gentle, but dominant wind accompanied by drizzle was first. Then the storm moved in. Rain was definitely a factor, but the wind was the major constituent. We made our way immediately toward the clubhouse.

After the storm had calmed down, we noticed the damages.

There were obvious physical damages of broken golf carts, muddy grips, and soggy shoes. There were some other damages much greater than the physical damages. That damage was the injury to our pride. We had stopped playing golf because of the weather.

#3
From Dust to Dust

Guiding Purpose: My guiding purpose is to describe my experience of going to Aunt Julia's funeral.

I. The death of Aunt Julia made me feel very unhappy.
   A. Aunt Julia had been my favorite aunt.
   B. Her death surprised me, although it had been expected on many previous occasions.
II. The family service was very sad.
   A. One small grandchild cried pitifully for the return of her grandmother.
   B. Uncle Jonathan, Julia's husband, was almost in a state of shock.
III. The congregational service was a tremendous experience for me.
   A. Sadness and mourning still prevailed.
   B. Reverend Smart's sermon brought strength to almost everyone.
   C. The congregational singing aroused a melancholy feeling within me.
   D. The service ended much too soon.
IV. The saddest experience of my life was when I attended the graveside service for Aunt Julia.
   A. A blizzard was in progress.
   B. When Reverend Smart placed the small handful of clay on the casket, tears formed in my eyes.

The small delegation of mourners walked slowly toward their cars. The violent, bitter blizzard seemed to rage more viciously now than it had during the funeral service. Even though Julia had been my favorite aunt, the fact still remained that she was now making intimate peace with her Father. I was glad for her, but I was also deeply saddened.

Julia had been an educated woman, but she still had enjoyed the simple gossip of our small town. She had been sick most of her life from such ailments as appendicitis, ulcers, diabetes, and cancer. Her death had been expected on many occasions, but when she finally died of a heart attack, everyone was surprised.

The family service for her, which was held in the Schneider

Funeral Parlor, was very sad. The sound of the whispering music combined delicately with the fragrance of the elegant roses to establish a very somber effect. Uncle Jonathan, Julia's husband, held his handkerchief to his eyes with his right hand. He had lost his other in a gruesome accident when he was picking corn. Hypertension painted his grieving cheeks purple. Four year-old Annie cried pitifully for the return of her grandmother; however, her plea was met only by Mr. Schneider, who quietly and patiently closed the lid of the bronze-colored coffin.

The congregational service in remembrance of Julia was somewhat repetitious because sadness and mourning again prevailed. Reverend Smart pointed out that death was a part of God's will and that we had no reason to question His will. He admitted that the presence of death usually instilled sadness for the survivors. For the person who had died, however, death was an experience greater than life itself. The family had braced itself somewhat by this time, but when the congregation sung the traditional anthem, "Rock of Ages," another torrent of sorrow fell upon the family. After we had left the church, we found that a blinding blizzard was in progress. We shuffled toward the cemetary.

The cold crept under the sides of the fluttering tent. Reverend Smart, who offered a prayer of comfort, was heard by hardly anyone. The only thing that was important to us was to get relief from the unbearable cold situation. When Reverend Smart scooped a small handful of clay from the ground and placed it on the casket, however, our own selfish motives were forgotten. We would never see Julia again. A small tear formed in every eye, and a lump grew in every throat as the small delegation of mourners walked slowly toward their cars.

#4
Christmas Crisis
Guiding Purpose: My family was unified one Christmas Eve when Mother was sick.
 I. All the members of the family were present.
   A. We were opening our gifts.
   B. Everyone was having a good time.

II. Mother suddenly got sick.
   A. She tried not to show her pain.
   B. We thought she was having a heart attack.
   C. We tried to comfort her.
   D. We worked together when we cleaned the living room.
III. This was the best and most dramatic Christmas that I have ever experienced.
   A. When the crisis came, we assumed our responsibilities without thinking.
   B. It was great because our efforts were unified for the first time in many years.

    The favorite carols had been warbled by the church choir and had been chanted by the monotones at the Christmas Eve service, in such a manner that the rasps from the monotones completely overshadowed the perfect coldness of the good birds. The traditional, brown, rum-soaked monster had been attacked and devoured, but from the way that most of us felt, we reluctantly conceded that we had actually lost the battle. Our family was enjoying a Christmas Eve together. We moved into the living room with anticipation and fear. Were the presents in those deceivingly wrapped packages really what we wanted, or would most of them go into the gift rack, a place where unwanted presents were kept until an opportunity arose to pass them on to some other unfortunate prey? The ribbons, strings, and tape were gradually thrown about the chamber, and we found that they had concealed such items as stuffed monkeys; three bottles of after-shave lotion; and one, noisy, white petticoat. I received some very valuable gifts, but I also received some completely useless gifts. I was sure that finding a dozen handkerchiefs in one carton was ridiculous. Generally, we were happy and pleased, though.
    Everyone was thoroughly enjoying himself, when Mother suddenly dropped out of the casual conversation and general gaiety. We thought she had merely gone to the kitchen to begin preparing some cold turkey for lunch. When we went out to investigate, however, she was as white as a plaster of Paris statue of an angel that I had seen in church. We asked her if anything was wrong, but she said that she must have indulged too much in the Christmas feast. Then she sat down as though she were going to faint. The corners of her mouth quivered slightly, even though her lips were locked together

tightly. We thought she may have had a heart attack. My sister cried, not because her Christmas festivities had been ruined, but because she hated to see her mother go through such agony. My brother-in-law and Dad helped her into the bedroom. She lay almost as quietly and as rigidly as the crisp, white sheets. After Dad had courageously fought his way through the wilderness of paper and ribbons, he reached the phone to call Dr. Perkins. The bones of the cold bird still lay on the China platter. My sister began to clean up the living room. My little nephew also reluctantly started to match his new toys with their respective boxes. Dr. Perkins finally arrived, and he looked as though he were thoroughly sorry for ever taking up this profession. He walked into the bedroom and began an examination. Almost immediately he announced that she was suffering from a gallstone attack. The doctor's proclamation brought relief within us, but it only meant pain for Mother.

That was a tremendous Christmas. Each of us had been enjoying life in his own selfish way. When unfortunate luck came, however, we assumed our responsibilities seriously. Yes, a few worthless stones converted a small reunion of human beings into a unified family.

#5
The Search

Guiding Purpose: It was myself I searched for, my identification among two billion people, my stamp of uniqueness (if anything actually existed).

I. Without significance
   A. Searching for myself
   B. Slipped away like a thief in the night
II. Changeable visions
   A. Clear and pure as blue sky
   B. Hazy, floating, drifting
III. Object of search in different places
   A. Shade of an oak tree
   B. Noisy battlefield
   C. Comfort of home
   D. Couldn't touch it
   E. Knew I would find it

It was as if I were not I, but another creature of the night. Without name, face, or significance, I was carried automatically toward some unknown destination. I searched for something just beyond my reach. When my hand grasped for it, it slipped away like a thief in the night.

I could see it in my mind; but it was so changeable that it took me several seconds to realize that this was what I was searching for. It was scarred and ugly, tattered and torn beyond recognition. It was as clear as the blue sky over the sun drenched meadow. It was hazy, floating, drifting in many forms.

It lay in some quiet pasture; in swift moving waters; on a blood spattered battlefield; in the comfort of home. It lay everywhere, just within reach. But I couldn't touch it, for it slithered from my grasp. Where could I find it? And most important, when?

#6
The Conflict

Guiding Purpose: How I felt when my friends and my teacher eyed me critically because I failed to dress properly for one "dress-up day."

I. I was against having to wear my best clothes to school.
   A. I thought the idea was ridiculous.
   B. I was certain that the way in which the idea was brought about was unjust.
II. I came to school in the morning of the big day dressed in very unorthodox clothing.
   A. I wore every obnoxious combination of clothing that I could think of.
   B. Teachers and classmates eyed me critically.
   C. I kept my composure, because I felt that I was struggling for my rights.
III. I suffered from the incident.
   A. I was nearly expelled from school.
   B. My struggle failed miserably.

Faint sounds, like those from the inhabitants of a Montana pasture, seemed to accompany the enthusiastic gestures of the raised, pink hoofs that were possessed by the members of the Sophomore class. There wasn't supposed to be any way of avoiding the situation. Everyone had to wear their finest clothing to school for a day. I had shown the class several good reasons why a dress-up day was very foolish. Wearing a suit in an industrial arts class would be confronting the owner with a dry cleaning bill, because attending church in a saw-dust-covered suit is not widely accepted. A suit of clothing would assuredly look really fresh after it had been folded and placed in a wire basket while the suit owner practiced the hook shot. Accidentally spilled ink would certainly add several informal touches to an expensive silk tie. However, the president of the class was unanimously in favor of wearing his new corduroy suit to school, and his followers thought that such a day would enable them to appear very desirable to their steady mates. Thus, a dress-up day was proclaimed.

The morning of the tragic day arrived. I decided not to be so obstinate as to wear a sweat shirt and a pair of jeans. I figured that I would meet the minimum requirements of dress, a suit and a necktie, in a dissenting manner. Being donned in a green shirt, a pair of brown trousers, a white tie, a pair of white shoes, and a black suit coat was overdoing it, though. An atmosphere with heavy dark clouds in it formed within a half hour after I had arrived at school. A few seconds later a torrent of emotion, from hysterical laughter to war-like contempt, fell. Teachers and students eyed me critically. I kept trying to tell myself that I hadn't really seen my government teacher throw an eraser at me. The weather was far from fair, so many of my friends failed to help me or to recognize me. I was pushed to the back of the lunch line by Mr. Williams, the principal. When I finally reached the lunchroom, I noticed that the faculty members were sitting around the first table with frowns on their faces. I crept to the third table with my fish sticks and my white necktie. There was an anxious lull in the storm, almost like that of stopping a war to participate in the Greek Olympics. After lunch, a fearful gale moved in. My English teacher would not recognize my physical response to a question, even though none of my classmates had his hand raised. My biology teacher forced me to take a test two days before any other person had to take the examination. I kept my composure, even though I was gravely abused, because I still thought that I was struggling for a very meaningful cause. The sun finally broke through the violent storm at four o'clock, but sprinkles of oppression fell like a fall-out for many days afterward.

I heard afterward that I had nearly been expelled from school for my contrary behavior. I found that I had failed miserably in my one man cause. My only real accomplishment from this incident was that I had made a fool of myself. Like a Kiowa Indian, I realized that my rights were being stolen from me. Consequently, in order to protect myself from more embarrassment and abuse, I decided to bury the hatchet. When another dress-up day was proclaimed, I went promptly to the cemetary to repossess my cause; but as I opened the grave, I found my opponents' hatchet, also. The next day, I wore my black suit, a white shirt, and a conservatively colored tie to school.

---

3. Exposition

#1
Television is Good

Guiding Purpose: My purpose is to tell why I think television is good.
  I. Entertainment
     A. Professional quality
     B. Variety and sports
 II. Education
III. Future television
     A. Improvement
     B. Quality

"I think I'll just stay home and watch television tonight." This is a familiar quote all over the country. In the past ten years television has grown until it is now the largest single family entertainment in the United States. Television has also been deemed by many as the biggest boon to education since the introduction of the printed page. I'm inclined to agree with both of these statements.

Through television, people are able to see how the majority of other people live. They are no longer confined to their own back yards. Television, now with the aid of the Telestar satellite, enables the public to see televised subjects from all over the world. "Sunday Sports Spectacular," for example, allows the television viewer to watch the best athletes perform. This same thing is true in reference to variety entertainment. The "Ed Sullivan Show" has for years presented some of the greatest performers from Broadway and Hollywood to the television audience. I think everyone would agree with me that nothing is more relaxing and pleasant than sitting home and watching one's favorite comedian or singer.

In the field of education, today's television offers several programs with educational backgrounds. "The Twentieth Century" is an interesting and informative presentation of recent history. "C.B.S. Reports," on the other hand, is an up-to-date synopsis of current events. Both of these programs are extremely fine examples of television's value as an educational factor. In the future, I think and hope that more and more television programs will be patterned after these.

In closing, I must admit that other types of television programs exist, but these are not fit to be included on the same level as those I have previously mentioned. This type too is thriving with large audiences, but this audience demands violence and bloodshed instead of excellence. I only hope that in the future as the American people progress intellectually they will demand and recieve "good" television programs.

Section VIII

#2
My Favorite

Guiding Purpose: My purpose is to tell why I think Ernest Hemingway is a great writer.

I. Hemingway
   A. Great writer
   B. Books
II. Hemingway's style
   A. Sentences
   B. Effectiveness
   C. Emotion

In my opinion, the late Ernest Hemingway is one of the greatest writers of the past century. His books have been translated and are now read all over the world. Two of his works, *The Old Man and the Sea* and *For Whom the Bell Tolls*, are my favorites from all the modern novels that I have read.

What impresses me most about Hemingway is his ability to take simple people and common occurrences and convey them to the reader with feeling and warmth. By taking ugliness and brutality and mixing it with the problems of the lives of his characters, Hemingway creates beauty in the mere existence of man. This unique ability allows him to relate the entire story in short, meaningful sentences. While other writers may bore the reader with facts, Hemingway can deal with the minutest details without tiring the reader. These are all part of Hemingway's style of writing. They are what made his works great and what makes me get the odd but wonderful feeling that I felt after finishing *For Whom the Bell Tolls*.

#3
Shoot-Um Shows

Guiding Purpose: To show by means of illustration that, because adult westerns are much the same as westerns for children, the popularity of western television shows is great.

I. Little boys' television show
 A. Masked rider and Indian friend
 B. Mystery, excitement, shooting
 C. Johnny's favorite
II. Father chuckling at son's show
 A. Lone Ranger—kid stuff
 B. Tunes in his favorite show
III. Scene of gambling casino
 A. Glamour of casino
 B. Bret attracted by blonde
 C. Thompson brothers after Maverick
IV. Comparison of child's western and adult western
 A. Same thing
 B. Add blonde, casino, and comedy to youngsters' western to get adult show
 C. Reap audience twice as big
 D. Boys and men have same sense of excitement

The saddled palomino galloped his masked rider across the open plain toward a secluded grove where he was to meet an Indian friend. The job they had to do was unknown to the small boy who sat Indian-style, eyes fastened on the twenty-one inch screen which blazed forth his favorite shoot-um show. The mystery of the masked man's identity, the excitement offered by his narrow escapes with death, and the constant blazing of guns all combined to make "The Lone Ranger" Johnny's favorite television show.

As the Lone Ranger and Tonto disappeared in the shadows of the evening, the boy's mother called, "Time for bed, Johnny!" Before leaving the room, Johnny grinned at his father and said, "Boy, that sure was a good show, Dad. You should watch it sometime!" His father chuckled to himself and turned on his favorite program. "The Lone Ranger," he thought. "Kid stuff!" The man settled himself comfortably in the overstuffed armchair as the show began.

Sparkling chandeliers hung from the ceiling of the gambling casino, mirrors lined the walls, and a deep red carpet covered the large floor. Potential gamblers and professional card sharks swarmed around the roulette wheels, black jack tables, and dice cages. A dark haired man by the name of Bret roamed among them. His eyes were attracted by a shaply blonde in a spangled dress. As he wandered toward her, guns were fired from the outside and a bullet shattered the glass of the front window. Horses galloped quickly away. "The Thompson brothers have found me again," thought Bret as he pulled the blonde to safety. "Guess this time I'll have to fight 'em. Not that I'm scared, of course. It's just that I hate to kill a man."

And on it goes. . . .

Adult westerns are, essentially, the same as westerns made for young boys. All the producers need to do is add a shapely blond, a deck of cards, and a bit of comedy to the excitement, mystery, and shooting in order to reap an audience of at least twice as many viewers. Producers realize that grown men were once youngsters with much of the same enthusiasm for excitement. As they grow older their ideas of excitement change, but they have the same basis. So all the producer has to do is add the foundation to make his viewing audience grow. And he does.

#4
To Attain Greatness

Guiding Purpose: To attain greatness—that peak of achievement whereby a man is worthy of highest esteem—one must do more than possess characteristics, such as strength of will and self-confidence, that are attributed to great men: he must by actual deed or inspiring leadership cause mankind to be safer, as by promotion of peace or eradication of disease; happier, perhaps through creation of outstanding music or painting; or freer, as in abolition of tyranny.

I. How does a man reach greatness—that peak of achievement whereby one is worthy of highest esteem?
   A. He does not gain it by merely possessing certain characteristics attributed to great men; to be strong in will or desirous to remake society is not enough.
   B. If a man is to gain eminence, it seems to me, he ought to use his abilities and ideas toward accomplishing some noteworthy goal: He must do something.
   C. To discover how greatness may be attained, let us consider certain areas of action in which men have distinguished themselves.
II. Men have rendered considerable service by making the world safer for mankind.
   A. Those who have worked tirelessly to keep pace with the world are worthy of our highest regard.
   B. Leaders in the fight to eradicate disease are certainly to be honored.
      1. Men like Louis Pasteur and Dr. Jonas Salk have labored to give us protection from raging epidemics.
      2. Medical people who risk their lives today in disease-ridden parts of the world like Africa and Asia have attained a kind of greatness.
      3. Perhaps this is the noblest kind when they sacrifice their own lives that other people may go on living.
III. There are men who have reached distinction by producing artistic beauty.

    A. Shakespeare's plays continue to hold a high place in world literature.
    B. The masterpieces in painting are thrilling to millions.
    C. Time has not touched the beauty or magnificence of compositions by Beethoven, Chopin, or Mozart.
    D. The creators of these works have attained greatness, for they have promoted happiness and tranquility by causing men to reflect upon aesthetic matters.

IV. Surely some of the men most deserving of reverence are those who have battled for freedom.
    A. We immediately recall the early patriots, Paul Revere, John Hancock, George Washington, and others, who by actual deed and inspiring leadership made the Revolutionary War a victory.
    B. In addition, we honor American soldiers of later wars; how many there have been, like Roger Young, who sacrificed their lives to save their loved ones and the democratic ideals on which this country was built.
    C. Throughout history there have been men of greatness who have worked to abolish tyranny.

V. These examples of greatness are not complete, to be sure, but I believe that they indicate what one must do to reach a position of eminence.
    A. This point is attained when a man does something that makes life better for other men.
    B. He achieves distinction when he has placed others' welfare before his own in carrying out a deed.
    C. The life of one who has attained greatness serves to improve the world and the lot of mankind.

How does a man reach greatness—that peak of achievement whereby one is worthy of highest esteem? He does not gain it merely by possessing certain characteristics attributed to great men. To be strong in will or desirous to remake society is not enough. If a man is to gain eminence, it seems to me, he ought to use his abilities and ideas toward accomplishing some noteworthy goal. To discover how greatness may be attained, let us consider certain areas of action in which men have distinguished themselves.

Men have rendered considerable service by making the world safer for mankind. Those who have worked tirelessly to keep pace with the world are worthy of our highest regard.

Leaders in the fight to eradicate disease are certainly to be honored. Men like Louis Pasteur and Dr. Jonas Salk have labored to give us protection from raging epidemics. Medical people who risk their lives in parts of Africa and Asia to eliminate ravaging diseases have attained a kind of greatness. Perhaps this is the noblest kind when they sacrifice their lives that other people might go on living.

There are men who have reached distinction by producing artistic beauty. Shakespeare's plays continue to hold a high place in world literature. The masterpieces in painting are thrilling to millions. Time has not touched the beauty or magnificence of compositions by Beethoven, Chopin, or Mozart. The creators of these works have attained greatness. They have promoted happiness and tranquility by causing men to reflect upon aesthetic matters.

Surely some of the men most deserving of reverence are those who have battled for freedom. We immediately recall the early patriots, Paul Revere, John Hancock, George Washington, and others, who by actual deed and inspiring leadership made the Revolutionary War a victory. In addition, we honor the American soldiers of later wars. How many there have been, like Roger Young, who sacrificed their lives to save their loved ones and the democratic principles on which this country was built. Throughout history there have been men of greatness who have worked to abolish tyranny.

These examples of greatness are not complete, to be sure, but I believe that they indicate what one must do to reach a position of eminence. This point is attained when a man does something that makes life better for other men. He achieves distinction when he has placed others' welfare before his own. The life of one who has attained greatness serves to improve the world and the lot of mankind.

#5
Death and Pain

Guiding Purpose: The effect of a specific happening on human emotion and how it changes as the conditions under which it is viewed change, is vividly illustrated in Samuel Pepys's "Diary of a Plague Year."

I. Most people feel uneasy at the sight of a human corpse or another human in pain, but if a person sees death and pain of certain causes often enough, he will become accustomed to it and it will not bother him a great deal.
   A. Medical doctors whose job it is to preserve life are not as affected by death as most people.
   B. Ambulance drivers very seldom feel squeamish when they are seeing a badly mangled body because they see mutilated humans almost everyday.
   C. Seeing dead bodies is an everyday event to a mortician who must deal with death as his means of making a living.
II. The same person can view the same type of event, such as pain or death, and it will effect him differently depending on the circumstances surrounding the incident.
   A. In "Diary of a Plague Year," Pepys viewed human pain, he saw it with two completely different types of emotion.
      1. He was not affected by death due to the plague because it had become common to see many dead bodies everyday.
      2. The pains of the sailors due to their lack of money bothered him because their pain was not necessary and should not have taken place.
   B. As in the death of a relative, a person feels grief for the deceased person, yet if the dead person was not known, his death would mean nothing to the people not close to him.
III. As illustrated by these examples, a person's reaction to death or pain depends upon, besides on the individual, the circumstances surrounding the incident, not the actual occurrence itself.
   A. Pepys thought about death with two different emotions because he saw death under two completely different emotions.
   B. For these reasons, I feel that the way a person reacts to a situation depends on the frequency with which it is seen and the circumstances surrounding the event.

Most people feel uneasy at the sight of a human corpse or another human in pain, but if a person sees death and pain due to certain causes often enough, he will become accustomed to it and it will not bother him a great deal. Medical doctors whose job it is to preserve life are not as affected by death as most people. Ambulance drivers very seldom feel squeamish when they see a badly mangled body, whereas other people might, because they see mutilated humans almost everyday. Seeing dead bodies is an everyday event to a mortician who must deal with death as his means of making a living.

The same person can view the same type of event, such as pain or death, and it will affect him differently depending on the circumstances surrounding the incident. In "Diary of a Plague Year," Pepys viewed the humans' pain with two completely different types of emotion. He was not affected by death due to the plague because it had become common for him to see many dead bodies everyday. The pains due to the starving of the sailors due to their lack of money bothered him because their pain was not necessary and should not have taken place. As in the death of a relative, a person feels grief for the deceased person, yet if the dead person was not known personally, his death would mean nothing to the people not close to him.

As illustrated by these examples, a person's reaction to death or pain depends, besides the individual, on the circumstances surrounding the incident, not the actual occurrence itself. Pepys thought about death with two different types of emotion because he saw death under two completely different conditions. For these reasons I feel that the way a person reacts to a situation as discussed in this theme depends on the frequency with which it is seen and by the circumstances surrounding the event.

#6
Our World

Guiding Purpose: I believe the statement—"God gave the world to men in common; but since he gave it to them for their benefit, and the greatest conveniences of life they were capable to draw from it, it cannot be supposed He meant it should always remain common and uncultivated"—is logical.

I. I believe that God gave the world to us for our benefit.

      A. Why would He allow the world to grow?
      B. When evil increased too much he destroyed.
      C. The world grew again.
II. Our conveniences
      A. Natural resources
      B. Conveniences in life
III. Will remain changing
      A. He is allowing us to try to conquer space.
      B. We are gaining knowledge in many fields.
      C. There have been many changes.
IV. This is our world
      A. Until evil takes over
      B. He ended the world once with a flood, next time it will be a fire.

I believe, the statement—"God gave the world to men in common; but since He gave it to them for their benefit, and the greatest conveniences of life they were capable to draw from it, it cannot be supposed He meant it should always remain common and uncultivated."—is logical. He gave it to us for our benefit. He has allowed the world to grow from the time he put Adam and Eve on it to the present world that we live in. During that time evil became so terrible that he had one man, Noe, build an Ark that would hold a female and a male of every species. The rains came and flooded the world leaving the specimen on the Ark to remake the world, which has been growing since. He gave us Ten Commandments to live by. A Son that died for our sins was also given.

The world we live in has many natural resources that allow us to live easier. These are soils that are producing abundant crops and foods to take care of the people. The mind that we were given is developing and we are learning to take care of our soil and other resources. Some of our minerals in the earth are becoming exhausted but we are learning to find and use other minerals and elements in the earth. Sometimes part of our resources are lost from carelessness, but rules and safety men, watching for dangers, are trying to protect our resources. We have many conveniences to allow us to live easier. We have nations with governments to protect the people. In this country most people have homes to live in and jobs, if they want them, to support themselves. There are many recreational facilities which allow one to have fun and enjoy life.

God is allowing us to go further. Our minds are creating new means of travel. We are starting to conquer space and we will try in time to reach other planets. Beside gaining knowledge in the space fields of science, we are constantly conquering once harmful diseases. While learning more about our complex bodies and the world there are always new things coming up and being invented for the men of the future to learn about. On the farm and in the city there have been many changes just in my lifetime.

God created the world for us and He will allow us to live on it until we forget that He once sent a Son to this earth to die for our sins. When we forget that Jesus lived for us and evil and sin take over our minds, God will create a great fire that will destroy the world and allow him to create a new world with new people.

#7
Language and Politics

Guiding Purpose: Within the past month three important political figures—Fidel Castro, Defense Secretary Robert McNamara, and Charles DeGaulle—have made use of the hackneyed phrases, pretentious diction, and meaningless words associated with the decline of language to deceive their people into accepting a favorably slanted impression of the well-being of their country.

I. Modern language is on the decline, becoming cluttered with hackneyed phrases, pretentious diction, and meaningless words.
   A. Examples
      1. Hackneyed phrases
      2. Pretentious diction
      3. Meaningless words
   B. Results
      1. Loss of conciseness
      2. Greater opportunity for misunderstanding
   C. Importance of results
II. Earlier this month Fidel Castro celebrated the fifth anniversary of his Cuban revolution.
   A. Quote from the *Times*

B. Actual state of his country
C. Implied meaning by Castro is deceptive
III. Here in the United States, Barry Goldwater, campaigning in New Hampshire, expressed dissatisfaction with the Democratic defense policy.
A. Goldwater's statement about the dependability of our missiles
B. McNamara's statement implies the opposite
C. McNamara's statement is deceptive
IV. But perhaps the most interesting statement is that made by Charles deGaulle.
A. Purpose of the statement
B. The statement
C. Criticism of the language
V. Many other examples of the abuse of language can be found in almost every political statement.
A. The language does not promote understanding.
B. Misunderstanding promotes chaos.

Modern language is on the decline, becoming cluttered with hackneyed phrases, pretentious diction, and meaningless words. For example, worn-out metaphors are used to save the trouble of inventing new ones, statements padded to give an impression of elegance or intellectuality, terms are used inaccurately to describe a subject to which they are in no way related, and words with variable meanings are employed in one way to mislead the reader who assumes the second interpretation. The result of this corruption of the language is a loss of conciseness and increased opportunity for misunderstanding. These factors are important wherever communication is essential, because they limit its effectiveness, especially in politics if, as Orwell states, "all issues are political issues." A citizen must be able to express his wishes to his representative, the politician seeking election has to impart his convictions convincingly, and one country's statesmen need to deal in clear, concrete terms with the leaders of other countries to promote friendly relationships. But the inaccuracies of our modern language allow political speeches and statements to conform to the party line, praising and defending party policies at all costs. Deception becomes easy and lies appear acceptable. Three examples of misuse of language are important in recent events.

Earlier this month Fidel Castro celebrated the fifth anniversary of the Cuban revolution. At a large rally he quoted a statement from the *New York Times* which declared that "the Castro regime is certainly strong and possibly stronger than ever." True as the statement may be, it has little to do with the condition of the country or its people. Actually, the Cuban economy is dropping steadily. Men and women are drafted for forced labor in the fields, wages are being lowered, and food is rationed. Mis-management and a hurricane reduced the 1963 crop to the lowest in twenty years. Castro used the term "strong" to indicate prosperity and serve his purpose of promoting the regime, while the *Times* probably referred to power.

Here in the United States, Barry Goldwater, campaigning in New Hampshire, expressed dissatisfaction with the Democratic defense policy of increased dependence on intercontinental missiles instead of bombers. He stated, "I don't feel safe at all about our missiles. I wish the Defense Department would tell the American people how undependable the missiles in our silos actually are." He could not reveal this information, of course, because it is classified. But in Washington the Secretary of Defense, Robert McNamara, quickly protested that he was "Shocked" by Goldwater's remark and termed the statement "completely misleading, politically irresponsible, and damaging to the national security." Superficially, McNamara's announcement negated Goldwater's charge. The Defense Secretary, however, had done little more than say that Goldwater had no right to tell the American people and the people of other countries that the United States may not be as good as they are supposed to think she is. He did not flatly deny the charge.

But perhaps the most interesting statement is that made by Charles De Gaulle several weeks ago after delivering a major policy speech to the French people. His purpose was to convince his countrymen that they were never so prosperous and to assure them that progress is inevitable. He made this remark to newsmen: "The whole world is calm now. Even the Chinese are trotting around." Although the word "calm" is a relative term, it would be difficult to think of the world as calm. At the time of De Gaulle's speech, Greeks and Turks were slaughtering one another in Cyprus. And the reference to the Chinese as "trotting around" is hardly accurate and even ridiculous.

Many other examples of the abuse of language can be

found in almost every political statement. Like Castro, McNamara, and De Gaulle, political leaders can easily use vague phrases to their own advantage, and eventually one begins to doubt the sincerity of their speeches. This doubt is often the cause of the existing political chaos.

#8
The Effect of a Plague on Seventeenth Century Society

Guiding Purpose: A plague was a social crisis in the seventeenth century because people were driven to desperation as a result of lack of knowledge about the control and elimination of the disease.

I. During one plague in England in the seventeenth century, one thousand one hundred and fourteen bodies were thrown into a burial pit within two weeks.
   A. Infected people often buried themselves.
   B. Others, untouched by the disease, were affected by the sight of those who were stricken.
   C. Such desperation was caused by the hopelessness of coping with the disease.
      1. There was no way to eliminate it.
      2. There were few means of controlling it.
   D. The large numbers of deaths damaged the society.
   E. But more important was the social crisis caused by wide-spread desperation.

II. When a plague struck in the seventeenth century, there seems to have been little that could be done to mitigate the destruction it caused.
   A. Infected persons and their families were quarantined.
   B. There was a strict order to keep people from the pits.
   C. Infected persons were put to bed and sweated.
   D. These actions had little effect upon control of the disease.
      1. So many people were killed.
      2. Despair runs through accounts of the plague years.

III. One reason for this lack of effectiveness was the lack of scientific and medical knowledge necessary to cure the victims and protect others.
   A. Laws were not rigidly enforced.

B. Realizing the futility of fighting the plague, people attempted to escape from it.
      1. Families of infected persons could leave town before discovery by the officials.
      2. People broke out of quarantined homes.
   C. Those who did escape found their situation no better.
      1. Infected persons did not know what they were doing.
      2. Nobody believed the person who claimed to be well.
IV. The situation, then, became a vicious cycle.
   A. Desperation forced people to attempt to escape.
   B. Many people who escaped were infected and only spread the disease farther.
   C. In the end, no one trusted anyone else.
   D. Without a sound basis of trust, people cannot live together and coöperate.
   E. Without cooperation, the seventeenth century society could not hope to fight the plague effectively.
   F. Thus, the social crisis was created.

During one plague in England in the seventeenth century, one thousand one hundred fourteen bodies were thrown into a burial pit within two weeks. In their delirium, infected people near death often buried themselves by jumping into these pits. Others, untouched by the disease, were frightened out of their memories, their understanding, and even their lives by the sight of an infected relative. Such desperation was caused by the hopelessness of coping with the disease. Science and medicine had not progressed far enough to discover a way to eliminate these plagues, and there was also a lack of knowledge about means of control. The loss of such numbers of its members was, of course, a great threat to the society where everyone had a function. But even more important was the social crisis caused by widespread fear and desperation.

When a plague struck in the seventeenth century, there seems to have been little that could be done to mitigate the devestation it caused. Infected persons and their families were quarantined. Their homes were shut up and watchmen were appointed to guard them. These watchmen were publicly whipped if they allowed anyone to leave a house that had been shut up. There was also a strict order to keep spectators away from the burial pits. As far as medical attention goes, plague victims were put to bed and sweated. Judging from the number of people who died from these plagues and the despair running through accounts of plague years, these actions were not very effective in controlling the spread of the disease.

One reason for this ineffectiveness was the lack of scientific and medical knowledge necessary to cure the victims and protect those who had not yet become infected. Secondly, the laws could not protect those who were free from the disease, nor could anything be done to enforce them. The laws could not have been too rigidly enforced, because there are accounts by people who inspected the burial pits with no difficulty. And the fact that there were watchmen who had to be whipped indicates that quarantines could not be counted on either. So, realizing the futility of fighting the plague, people attempted to escape from it. Families of infected persons sometimes managed to leave town before discovery by officials. But often these people just carried the disease into the homes of those who took them in. The families who did not leave before their homes were quarantined were even more miserable. Horrible shrieks were heard from such houses. The sight of the dying victim and the knowledge that they were only exposing themselves intensified the escape efforts of the other family members. Many tried to bribe the watchmen or their neighbors. Others tried violence and threatened their guards. Those who did escape found their situation no better. Infected persons did not know what they were doing and perished either from want or from the violence of their sickness. The people who were not infected nevertheless found themselves in similar situations because no one would believe them.

The result was a vicious cycle. Desperation forced people to attempt to escape from infected areas. Yet many who escaped were infected and only spread the disease further. In the end, trust was almost completely lacking in the plague-ridden society. But without a sound basis of trust, people cannot live together and coöperate. And without coöperation, the seventeenth century society could not hope to fight the plague effectively. This disorganization created a real social crisis at a time when organization was needed most.

4. The Book Review

#1
A Review of *For Whom the Bell Tolls*

Guiding Purpose: The relationship between Robert Jordan and Maria in Hemingway's *For Whom the Bell Tolls* conveyed a definite meaning to me.

I. Background of the story
   A. Spanish Civil War
   B. Robert Jordan, man of the world
   C. Maria, the simple and innocent girl
II. Robert and Maria
   A. Their relationship
   B. Their meaning to each other
   C. Their dreams
   D. Their separation
III. What story meant to me
   A. Feeling
   B. Reality

Hemingway, in his novel, *For Whom the Bell Tolls*, writes of the beauty and simplicity of a love affair amid the ruthlessness and brutality of war. Robert Jordan, the American fighting for his beloved Spain, finds himself in a guerrilla band preparing to blow up a key bridge during the Spanish Civil War. This, however, is not the story. The story is that of Robert Jordan and the native girl in the guerrilla band, Maria.

Jordan and Maria are thrown together by the circumstances of war. He is a man of the world and has had many women before. She is a simple girl who has been beaten and raped by the enemy. Together, on the mountain side in the warm autumn sunlight, they have each other, and find the true meaning and fulfillment of love. Even in the uncertainty of their time, Jordan and Maria dare to dream of their future. He thinks of when they will be able to be together in a hotel with clean sheets and room service and when he'll be able to buy Maria pretty clothes. Maria, in her simplicity, dreams only of pleasing her "Roberto" by learning to cook and to mend his clothes. All of these thoughts are accompanied by the foreboding premonition that they will never be, but this is shut out of Robert's and Maria's mind.

Throughout their association the lovers aren't concerned with the complexities of normal life. They are concerned only with each other and the preservation of their love. There are no conflicts between Robert and Maria during their whole affair. Their relationship is perfect—perfect until the end when the bridge is blown up and the guerrilla band is forced to leave the badly wounded Jordan behind and takes Maria with them.

Thus, the two wandering people found themselves and each other, had a brief but passionate affair, and were forced apart again. They met with nothing and parted with nothing except the emotion and feeling which is love itself.

#2
Tortilla Flat

Guiding Purpose: Steinbeck's attitude toward his characters was objective and this attitude was reflected in his presentation of them.

I. Though Steinbeck's keen wit is apparent throughout this book, I don't think his attitude or purpose was to make his characters funny.

II. Steinbeck is very objective in his presentation of the characters.
  A. His objectivity implies that the traits of his characters are applicable to almost everyone.
  B. There are very few instances in which he adds comments to suggest his attitude.
  C. It seems as though he carefully describes the character, and then sits back to watch his readers work.

III. Steinbeck's objective description of the characters adds an unusual amount of realism to them.
  A. This realism comes from keen observation.
  B. With careful inspection, however, the reader can identify different types of people, but they are far from stereotyped characters.

If books with long, dull, involved titles or plots are your

pet peeve, then *Tortilla Flat* will certainly serve as a pleasant escape. The book could best be described as a collection of many incidents, from swiping money from a miser to supporting the children of a prostitute, from the lives of five eash-going *paisanos* who lived in the hill near Monterey, California. Since these incidents were quite dissociated, the characters and their traits were what maintained the unity of the book. Steinbeck presented these characters in many situations and then described their reactions. The book, then, was a character study.

In accordance with Steinbeck's keen cleverness, I think that his attitude was one of objectivity interwoven with some humor. However, just because he was objective doesn't mean that he was indifferent. For instance, when Danny bought a vacuum cleaner for Sweets Romirez, she reacted with thankfulness to Danny, but what was more important to her was that she moved five rungs up on the social ladder of Tortilla Flat. The amusing thing was that no electricity was to be found in Tortilla Flat, but she still cleaned her thread-bare rug, making sounds like that what she guessed to be an electric motor. Steinbeck merely related this incident in a simple manner, but much can be implied from it.

Steinbeck was also very objective in his presentation. By this I mean that he carefully described the characters in a way as to portray a trait, but then he didn't usually indicate whether the trait was good or bad. Thus he didn't either exult or condemn his characters. There are a few instances when a phrase revealed his attitude, however. When the five friends were deciding whether or not to clean the bedroom windows of its dust and cobwebs is an example of such an instance.

Again the author merely related the incident and then sat back to let the reader interpret the passage for himself. The obvious interpretation is the reasoning of Pilar, one of the five friends. The only motivation for his comment was his scorn of work. The author's attitude was very objective, but his statement, "Pilar's sharp mind leaped to the problem with energy, but it was too easy for him," certainly provided a definite clue to the attitude of Steinbeck.

The really important aspect of Steinbeck's characters, that is the result of his objectivity, is the realism of the characters. Steinbeck formed characters and then developed them so carefully as to provide both a realistic character and a general character. In many instances, I could immediately assign the actions and reasons for action to some other real person, or to myself. However, because of Steinbeck's wit and originality, his characters did not become merely types. Even though different attributes could be assigned to each character, the fact still remained that they were low-class, drunken men who had little ambition to better themselves. Yes, Steinbeck's objective presentation came from keen and clever observation, not from projecting himself into the scene of the action.

Section IX

COMPOSITION AND LITERATURE: MAINTAINING A *SENSIBLE* BALANCE

1. The Role of Literature in the High School Composition Program
2. Critical Writing
3. What High School Literature is NOT
4. Suggestions for Maintaining a Sensible Balance

1. The Role of Literature in the High School Composition Program

Because the purpose of this manual is to emphasize the importance of the composition program within the context of the senior high school English curriculum, there heretofore has been little or no consideration of the teaching of literature—its methods and materials have been intentionally ignored for the sake of devoting attention to the specialized topics in the last eight sections. However, it is virtually impossible to neglect the teaching of literature or to presume that it can be eliminated from the composition program. To do so is to commit the same heresy practiced by those who would abolish the writing phase of the secondary English curriculum and concentrate entirely upon literature. The two disciplines are inseparable—literature is formulated and created by writers—and, as the heading of this section indicates, the only problem preventing a smooth fusion of the two is the inability of teachers and administrators to decide what they intend to do with the overall English program and to determine where the exphasis will be placed. Yet there is really no serious difficulty here; as this section will point out, a sensible balance between composition and literature *can* be resolved and maintained without the students having to sacrifice valuable time from the practice of their writing skills. But before this problem is examined in greater detail, it might be well to consider the area of the teaching of literature from the point of view of its value to the high school composition program.

First among the contributions of literature to writing is that it provides a plentiful store of ideas for student themes. Although teachers must always be concerned with theme topics that will enable students to express easily and readily ideas that are derived primarily from their own experiences and knowledge, a certain amount of imaginary wandering, if discriminately restrained, is beneficial even if it provides little more than variety. Any student who does not, as he reads, lie on the beach at Lilliput with Gulliver, ride in the joust with Ivanhoe, spurn the weakness of Godfrey Cass, admire the transformation of Henry Fleming, or rise to the passion of Marc Antony's rhetoric is, frankly, a victim of either serious abnormality or poor teaching. For within these passages and subsequent adventures are experiences that reflect the modern teenager's own ideas concerning life and the world in which he lives. Moreover, there is the romantic desire to be transported far beyond reality—the adult must read, dream, and then forget; the high school student can carry this vicarious experience one step farther by recording his dreams in the form of themes for composition class. If the silent and shy George Jones—sixth seat, fourth row—wishes to tear the wax from his ears and succumb to the treacherous wiles of the enchantress Circe, then permission certainly should be granted, for this one theme will undoubtedly be George's first and last chance to be exploited by a woman. However, his teacher must never allow George to storm Circe's lair at the expense of sacrificing the discipline of his written prose to the incoherent ramblings of his romantic and adventurous heart. Care should be taken to remind student writers that an idea, no matter how fanciful or imaginative, is still to be presented in a unified manner, as clearly and concisely as possible.

But not all theme topics taken from literary works need to be fantasies or romantic inventions. One of literature's most valuable contributions to young minds is that it provides students with the opportunity to combine their experiences with those of others who are older and possess the proper balance of discipline and creative imagination which enables their works to be regarded as models of good writing. If student-writers can be carefully trained to observe the better writers "at work"—to be able to see the formation of an idea and its subsequent development toward a definite conclusion—then they in turn develop an awareness of the necessity for perceiving what is good or bad in their own efforts. This may seem to appear as reverting to the ancient Greco-Roman system of teaching rhetoric, where young boys were trained to *imitate* mannerisms and stylistic devices of established writers and orators; however, this is *not* what is being advocated here. It is impossible to *imitate* a writer and produce what a critic or teacher would label as "original" writing. Yet it *is* possible for the young novice to *observe* the better characteristics of writers and their works and apply them to his own particular writing situation. For as his mind matures and his writing skill develops, the high school student will begin to conceive his own techinques of language and general writing mannerisms; he will develop a style based upon the recognition that those writers from the past who provided him with a basis for a beginning cannot totally assist him in a confrontation of his own personal ideas and experiences with the modern world in which he is both observer and contributor. He must proceed *independently* to record what he observes and experiences in a manner (style) that reflects not only the characteristics of proper writing discipline, but the sensitive imagination resulting from his own awareness to the living people and objects around him.

2. Critical Writing

Of primary concern in evaluating literature's role in the high school composition program is the effectiveness by which a novel, poem, play, or essay can "open the door" to certain *types* of themes. For example, there is the traditional "book report," the ageless thorn in the sides of both teachers and students. The purpose of this exercise has always been to encourage students to read independently of classroom supervision and influence. This in itself is a profitable lesson, but too often teachers are prone to relegate it to a mere completion of a blank form consisting of the title, author, characters, short statement of plot or author's purpose, and an equally short reader evaluation. In other words, a potential composition comprised of a student's judgment of a literary work and carefully substantiated with concrete, supporting details from the work itself has been reduced to a petty questionnaire for the purpose of determining whether or not a student has read a particular book. Of course teachers forget (or intentionally ignore) that any book report form can be completed merely by reading the book jacket and skimming the first chapter.

There is nothing seriously wrong with student criticism if it can be restricted to an elementary level, where it may serve as beneficial practice for work in expository writing. In a general area of student criticism, the young person reads a book and either likes or dislikes it. He then develops his composition from this reaction by citing concrete evidence from the work to substantiate his judgment or evaluation. Or, he may choose to limit his topic and concern himself with one or two major characters; he either likes or dislikes their actions, reactions, attitudes, or effect upon other characters. There is really no limit to which this simple form of critical judgment or evaluation can be reduced. The teacher can determine whether or not the work was read by how well the student supports his opinions.

But this type of writing does not have to be restricted to the book report; it can be applied to particular works that are studied in the classroom. No matter what the specific type of theme assignment, students need the opportunity to set forth honest evaluations of the literary works that they read, and in this form simple criticism is not harmful. It only becomes so when teachers insist that their students follow critical criteria far beyond their understanding and, in fact, far beyond the author's original intentions. Teachers must realize that scholarly criticism has no place in the high school English classroom, where it can only serve to confuse students who lack the education and maturity necessary to comprehend it.

Yet if it accomplishes nothing else, literature is a valuable companion to the high school composition program as a "change" from the more mechanical aspects of composition instruction. There are times when even the student-writer, like everyone who is devoted to the improvement of one skill or another, needs to abandon his own efforts and examine fresh avenues of approach. The teacher of composition is doing a great deal for his students by drilling them in organization, transition, development, purpose, and language and pursuing these formal presentations with intensive practice. Yet it is also beneficial for young writers to undergo periods of observation in order that they might see these theories skillfully activated by established writers of the past and present. This, naturally, coincides with the statements presented in Subsection 1 of this section regarding the training of students to see the better writers "at work." However, change for the mere sake of change has never been a valid philosophy in any discipline; these periods of observation, like the other phases of the composition program, must be carefully controlled so that every piece of literature under discussion has A DIRECT BEARING UPON SOME CONCRETE FACET OF THE WRITING TECHNIQUES that are being developed.

3. What High School Literature is NOT

Just as in any other problem—and maintaining a sensible balance between composition and literature is very definitely a problem—there is a negative aspect of the situation that needs to be exposed in order to gain a complete understanding as to why the difficulty exists. In the area of the teaching of literature at the high school level, these negative aspects are evident because too many English teachers have distorted definitions of literature that are automatically transferred to the classroom. The results are illustrations of what literature is *not* and how *not* to teach it to high school students. These negative results can be categorized into four major areas (although there are certainly more) which not only destroy attempts at a composition-literature balance, but also effectively hinder students' ability to achieve the perfection of their writing skill: (1) a study in symbolism and hidden meanings, (2) a biography lesson, (3) a heavy concentration on historical and general background material, and (4) an excuse for a vocabulary lesson.

Even to the most experienced and advanced student of literature, the study of symbolism is a nasty business. Its importance to the totality of understanding a literary work cannot be denied; what can be questioned, however, is its importance to the high school student in relation to the type of literature that he is reading. But of greater significance in the light of the supposed aims of the English curriculum at the secondary level is that to train students to seek out and interpret symbols in a poem, novel, or short story is a task that will require a considerable amount of time—time that will, out of necessity, have to be "borrowed without remuneration" from the writing phase of the curriculum. For prior to extracting and analyzing the symbols in a work of prose or poetry, students must first be taught to differentiate between *symbol* and *sign*, to separate *symbol* from *allegory* (almost a separate study by itself), and to fuse the two worlds with which most symbolists deal—the *finite* and the *infinite*. Then there are the various types of symbolism which need to be thoroughly explained and explored: *natural, private*, and *conventional* symbols. Finally, there is a need to understand and evaluate the major schools of symbolism in order to gain full appreciation of the numerous interpretations held by different writers and readers. The point that is being argued here, therefore, is not the validity for teaching symbolism as it pertains to literature, but *when* to teach it. The teacher who is prone to overestimate its value—and he can easily be categorized as an inexperienced instructor recently graduated from college—must pause to consider the intelligence level of his students. Intensive devotion to the study of symbolism can overpower the true meaning behind the complete product. Moreover, the interpretation of symbols in literature is a discipline reserved for the more intelligent and educated students at the undergraduate or graduate university level, not for the romantic and rather under-developed minds of high school adolescents. In the final analysis, then, the teaching of literature in the secondary school should be directed toward training students to interpret a poem or essay on the basis of what it means to *them*, rather than concern themselves with erudite discussions that have little merit and even less sense. But literature can only become valuable as an aid to teaching composition when inexperienced and veteran teachers with visions of false grandeur cease to act like third-rate literary critics.

The second category of malpractice, intentional or otherwise, that effectively distorts the teaching of literature exists when teachers place such a heavy emphasis upon biographical material that the work being studied is practically neglected. The unfortunate aspect of these biography lessons is that administrators and supervisors are easily deceived into believing that students are learning a great deal about literature through studies of authors' lives. The reason for this is that there are many "projects" that can be extracted from a mere encyclopedic entry as to give the appearance of actual learning. For example, a teacher can appoint a committee to deliver a report on the life of Samuel Johnson. Almost immediately, necessity requires the appointment of a sub-committee to report on the life of James Boswell, since everyone knows that one cannot be studied without considering the other. The next step is to divide the Johnson committee and the Boswell-sub-committee into additional sub-committees (the committee system has taken firm roots in the public schools) for the purpose of dealing with the various "phases" of these men's lives. What ensues is a "run" on the school library, unequalled since the class studied the last author, with heavy emphasis upon volumes "B" and "J" of the various encyclopedia permanently in residence. One or two classes later the several committees and subcommittees orally distribute this information to their wide-eyed audience, while teacher and administrator beam with satisfaction from the knowledge that the students are being trained in the methods and materials of research, not to mention public speaking. What is totally forgotten is that these projects can take days to prepare and present; to "cover" the literature text within the allotted time, the class will have to eliminate actual discussion of the *Lives of the Poets*, *The Life of Samuel Johnson*, or the *Dictionary* to provide the students who have not yet reported with a chance at the next author.

Closely allied with the biography lesson is the next evil, that which emphasizes such a heavy concentration upon "background material" that the work of literature is given even less of an opportunity of being presented for class discussion. This type of project is a far greater sin than the biography report, since there is absolutely no limit to the number of committees and subcommittees that can be formed. Just think what an enterprising teacher can do with Part I of *Gulliver's Travels* without ever having to refer to any portion of that work! In this part alone there are at least thirteen major items of background material or, to be more progressive about the situation, thirteen possible projects for student committees. These may include the following:

1. Political and religious implications of the beheading of Charles I
2. George I
3. Queen Anne
4. The War of the Spanish Succession and the Treaty of Utrecht
5. Whigs and Tories
6. Robert Harley and Viscount Bolingbroke
7. Jacobites
8. Sir Robert Wallpole
9. Orders of the Garter, the Bath, and the Thistle
10. The Earl of Nottingham
11. Religious struggles in England and France during the late seventeenth and early eighteenth centuries
12. The Test Act
13. The Committee of Secrecy

But in the event the teacher is not committee-minded, there is always the lecture method of presenting this material, guaranteed to confuse the students as to whether they are pursuing a course in English literature or English history. Of course it has not occurred to the advocates of background material that works such as *Gulliver's Travels* have endured the passage of time because historical references like those listed above are secondary to the true meaning of the author's purpose—a purpose that can only be discovered by actually reading the work itself. To do anything less is to evade the primary intentions of literature.

Finally, there is the tendency among those who teach literature at the secondary level to convert every assignment into a vocabulary lesson. This is perhaps the least of the evils created by misdirected teaching, since the words being studied *do* originate from the primary source. However, words are only effective within the context of a sentence or paragraph, and isolated drillwork in spelling and definition achieves nothing—only the same sterile results as overemphasis on isolated grammar in the teaching of writing. Yet this area *can* serve as an interesting and profitable study in etymology and usage that becomes increasingly effective in conjunction with discussions of the content of a literary work. Rather than waste time and energy on biographical and historical research, students can be introduced to the *Oxford English Dictionary*, taught to use it, and then given assignments in discovering the many changes that have taken place in their complex language—changes that are evident when words from a literary work written a century or two ago appear to convey meanings that are totally different from present usage. So language training is important to literature, and its use in the English class has a greater impact upon a student's education than daily spelling tests and drill-work in definitions.

4. Suggestions for Maintaining a Sensible Balance

A practical solution to maintaining a sensible balance between composition and literature is simply to offer two distinct courses, one in literature and the other in composition. But these two divisions *would not* be isolated from each other. Meeting regularly at the departmental level, English teachers would arrange syllabii for the various grade courses in order to insure unity in reading and writing assignments. There is no necessity for revising the units of study in composition and literature, since the only requirement is to remove the present syllabii and place them under the proper course heading. As far as the teaching staff is concerned, there need only be a realignment of duties insofar as designating those who are to teach composition and those who are to teach literature. But care must be exercised in clarifying the responsibilities for the assignment and reading of student themes. Not all of the writing is to be restricted to the composition phase of the program; the literature teacher will assign and read his own papers.

The distinct division occurs because the composition teacher handles the instruction of writing techniques and theory and is responsible for seeing that his students receive the required amount of writing practice necessary for the development of their writing skills. The literature teacher, on the other hand, is to be concerned with instruction in literary types, figures, and periods; he will direct his writing assignments toward the particular works being discussed in the course and estimate the value of these papers according to content and general writing ability. Any and all writing problems that he discovers in these papers that are *not* within the content of the literature course will be referred to the composition teacher, who in turn will discuss them with his class. In this manner, the unity of the two programs is maintained because the skills learned and practiced in the composition class are put to additional use and practice in the literature class. The students would receive the benefits of greater emphasis and knowledge of each area, a clear idea of what will be expected from each program, and additional writing practice beyond the traditional single theme-a-week.

There will be objections to such recommendations, but the most obvious barriers can be easily turned aside. First, there is the problem of placating teachers. To compensate for any undue discrimination in regard to which teachers would be responsible for literature and which for composition, a simple process of rotation can be established. A staff member would teach literature one year and composition the next, or the term of duty for each program can even be limited to one semester of each. Through this method, teachers become familiar with both phases of the entire English program. From the administrative point of view there will undoubtedly exist another problem, that of class scheduling. Since English is to be divided into two courses, another class period will have to be found. The "discovery" should not require much time, since there are two obvious alternatives: (1) eliminate one or two (or as many as needed) study halls and substitute them with recitation periods or (2) extend the school day by one class hour. But, if the possibility for one or the other of these alternatives is non-existent, the separate courses in composition and literature can still be attained without any undue hardship. A final alternative would be to schedule composition for three days per week and literature for the remaining two. This is not the most advisable solution, however, since the balance and equal emphasis allotted to each program becomes slightly out of proportion.

Obviously, therefore, if literature is to be instrumental in aiding the student-writers in the development of their writing skills, teachers and administrators must continue to remain alert to new methods whereby a more sensible balance between literature and composition *can* and should be maintained. The English curriculum at the senior high school level requires a complete reevaluation in order to eliminate the maze of clouded objectives which tradition and the academic world have forced upon it. Reading and writing are not easy skills for young minds to master; they must be developed progressively and thoroughly, yet clearly. Unless something is done to clarify these objectives so that students will be aware of what they must do for English and what English can do for them, the present decline in the reading and writing abilities of high school pupils is likely to extend to a depth far beyond recovery. For it is certainly more prudent to bring together what actually exists than to wait until complete disintegration ensues and precious time and money must be expended for reconstruction. Careful planning on the part of teachers and administrators *will* produce a high school English program constructed on the principle that students must learn to read and write within the full range of their abilities, and the program *will* be successful because the attention and emphasis placed upon these goals will have been sensibly balanced.

Section X

A SELECTED READING LIST FOR THE TEACHING OF HIGH SCHOOL COMPOSITION

Reading List

Prospective and in-service teachers of English composition would do well to examine the following list of articles and monographs in order to obtain further information concerning not only what will happen in the way of future writing programs at the high school level, but also to evaluate present methods and procedures. Practically every entry in this list is readily available from the National Council of Teachers of English (508 South Sixth Street, Champaign, Illinois) at very little cost.

A Language in Common. NCTE (reprinted from the *Times* (London) *Literary Supplement*).

Alm, Richard (ed.). *Books for You.* NCTE, 1964.

Basic Considerations for a New English Curriculum. Wisconsin Council of Teachers of English, Wisconsin State College, Oskosh.

Borgh, Enola M. *Grammatical Patterns and Composition.* NCTE.

Braddock, Richard, *et al. Research in Written Composition.* NCTE.

Brown, Rollo Walter. *How the French Boy Learns to Write.* Harvard University Press and NCTE.

Burke, Virginia M. *The Lay Reader Program: Backgrounds and Procedures.* Wisconsin Council of Teachers of English. Milwaukee, 1961.

—————. "The Lay Reader Program in Action." *Wisconsin Council of Teachers of English.* Special Bulletin No. 1 (November 1960).

Burrows, Alvina T., *et. al. Children's Writing: Research in Composition and Related Skills.* NCTE. Chicago, 1960-1961.

Burton, Dwight L. (ed.) *English Education Today*. NCTE.

──────────, *et al.* "A Check List for Evaluating the English Program in Junior and Senior High School." Reprinted from *The English Journal*, April, 1962.

Dendinger, Lloyd N. "High School Research Papers—A Waste of Time?" *Louisiana English Journal*, IV (Spring 1963), 27-28.

"Evaluating a Theme." *Newsletter of the Michigan Council of Teachers of English*, V, Spring, 1958.

"Evaluating Ninth Grade Themes." *Illinois English Bulletin*, XL, March, 1953.

"Evaluating Twelfth Grade Themes." *Illinois English Bulletin*, XL, April, 1953.

Friedrich, Edwin H. "Problems of Teaching Writing: A Basic Approach." *Louisiana English Bulletin*, IV (Spring 1963), 39-46.

Green, Milton, *et al.* "Standards for Written English in Grade 12." *Indiana English Leaflet*, III, October, 1960.

Hatch, Clarence W. "Needed: A Sequential Program in Composition." Reprinted from the *English Journal*, November, 1960.

Hook, J. N. "Grammar(s)—A Rationale." *Illinois English Bulletin*, LI (December 1963), 1-11.

Language, Linguistics, and School Programs. NCTE.

Loban, Walter. *The Language of Elementary School Children*. NCTE.

NCTE Committee on High School-College Articulation. "A Blueprint for Articulation." *College English*, XXIV (February 1963), 400-403.

Nail, Pat, *et al. A Scale for Evaluation of High School Student Essays*. NCTE, 1960.

Palmer, Orville. "Seven Classic Ways of Grading Dishonestly." NCTE (Reprinted from *English Journal*).

"Principles and Standards in Composition for Kentucky High Schools and Colleges." *Kentucky English Bulletin*, VI, Fall, 1956.

Promising Practices in the Teaching of English. NCTE, 1963.

Rogal, Samuel J. "College-High School Articulation: A Proposal." *CEA Critic*, XXVI (March 1964), 8-9.

Schueler, Donald G. "Programed Instruction and Teaching Machines." *Louisiana English Journal*, IV (Spring 1963), 29-34.

Squire, James, *et al. Basic Considerations for a New English Program*. NCTE.

Westmore, Thomas H. (ed.) *Linguistics in the Classroom.* NCTE.

Jewett, Arno and Charles E. Bish. *Improving English Composition*, NCTE.

Roberts, Paul. *English Syntax.* New York (Harcourt, Brace and World), 1964.

Allen, Harold B. *Readings in Applied Linguistics*, 2nd Ed. New York (Appleton-Century-Crofts), 1963.

Francis, W. Nelson. *The Structure of American English.* New York (The Ronald Press), 1958.

National Study of High School English Programs. *High School Departments of English.* NCTE.

Shugrue, Michael and George Hillocks. *Classroom Practices in Teaching English*, NCTE, 1965.

Brett, Sue M. *Supervision in English, K-12.* NCTE.

Lacampagne, Robert. *High School Departments of English: Their Organization, Administration, and Supervision.* NCTE.

Certainly no one can consider this small list to be a complete bibliography on recent trends in teaching composition. Rather, it is a starting point from which the reader can gather additional material from more detailed books, monographs, and articles. Also, if any teacher of composition is inclined toward discovering the activities of institutions, organizations, and individuals as they prepare to face the problems of the future of the composition program, he need only read his *English Journal*, one of the many professional periodicals that, unfortunately, has more subscribers than readers.

Section XI

THE FUTURE OF THE HIGH SCHOOL COMPOSITION PROGRAM

The Future of the High School Composition Program

The intense activity of academicians and educationists that has only recently begun to concern itself with the teaching of English in the high school (for example: Project English and the U.S. Office of Education-sponsored NDEA institutes) immediately raises one question: Why is the composition program in its present predicament and how did it ever get there in the first place? The answers are indeed plentiful—in fact practically all of them have been discussed throughout this book—but they can be reduced to three major problem areas: (1) too many students, (2) not enough teachers, and (3) the public's attitude toward education. Unfortunately, little or nothing can be done about the first problem; the only solution is to borrow, build, and borrow again when the latest building becomes too small. However, those connected with the English-teaching profession must visualize these huge enrollment figures not as student body totals, but in terms of thirty-six to forty themes per student per year. Then the problem automatically shifts to the second major area and becomes a simple matter of finding enough competent teachers to convey the principles of writing and to read these themes. However, something *can* be done about this just as soon as those now or about to be connected with education recognize that they belong to a profession; that a profession does not exist as such until it ceases to accept into its ranks derelicts from other fields of endeavor who believe that they can become successful teachers of English. Finally, the public must be made to recognize that teaching children to write is a professional matter that needs to be thoroughly planned and activated by competently trained professionals. When parents are permitted to dictate policy, then the English syllabus becomes a public relations manual. In other words, as long as parents and the general public can actually *see* what is happening in the school, they are content. But if the dispensing of knowledge requires no gimmicks or gadgets—merely the silent and traditional methods of placing words on a piece of paper—those on the outside become suspicious and fear that their children are not reaping the benefits of modernity. Therefore, once these barriers are removed, teachers and school administrators can concentrate on positive plans for the composition course of the future, and present predicaments hopefully will be substantially eased.

Yet those interested in improving the quality of student writing would be wise to consider suggested recommendations for the composition program that are applicable to the present, since this will constitute the foundation upon which future plans will be constructed. First, the many conferences, workshops, institutes, and curriculum study centers now in existence throughout the nation must continue to plan curricula and investigate methods by which school districts can maintain teaching staffs to handle increases in enrollments. Although conferences and planning sessions are time consuming, laborious, and often slow to produce definite results, the general problems of education and the specific area of the composition course are too intricate to be subjected to hasty decisions. Therefore, the present curriculum study centers must be expanded to include *all* levels and aspects of English education. Second, the advantages of instituting separate programs in literature and composition, as suggested in Section IX, are worthy of consideration, at least on a trial basis. There might even be merit in beginning this division at the elementary school level, where children will be able to understand immediately the importance of developing their reading and writing skills. As they advance to succeeding grade levels and arrive at the senior high school, the "image" of English will appear clearly as the continued development of these skills, rather than the present conglomeration of five or six areas of study presented at random. Finally, the senior high school composition program can be made to produce more positive and immediate results if curriculum planners continue to think in terms of a thirteen year course in writing—from grade one through freshman year of college. This is perhaps the best method for easing the sensitive problem of theme reading, especially for teachers of senior high school and college freshman English. *Any* child who is exposed to the principles of disciplined prose writing at age six—and this exposure is continued during each week of his education—certainly ought to be in command of his writing skills by the time he graduates from high school. For if *serious* training in language structure and composition is begun early, then teachers of senior high school composition will be able to *read* papers, rather than waste countless hours *correcting* them. But for this "continuous" program in composition to be successful, it will be necessary to eliminate the progressive attitude that the elementary school is a juvenile social parlor and revert to the philosophy that youngsters should spend their school hours learning, not playing.

Evidently, if some medication is not applied to relieve the pressures from high enrollments and teacher shortages upon the high school composition program, the breach will become irreparable and the teaching of writing non-existent. The only solution remains with those who are now members of the English teaching profession and with college students who are preparing to enter it. If English teachers are content to be mere spectators while school administrators and education theorists plan their programs for them, then they deserve every television set and movie projector that is thrust upon them. But if they are sincerely interested in fulfilling their professional responsibilities—responsibilities that extend far beyond the limits of their classrooms—then they will demand and assume a more active role in planning the present and future composition programs. Teachers are, in a sense, no different from elected governmental officers in that they are servants of the society which they represent. As long as the present society demands that students be able to write in a disciplined manner, teachers must instruct them to do so. If, during some time in the future, these demands are altered, then the present course of action will have to yield to other objectives. But at this moment the objectives are clear: students can only be taught to write through continuous writing practice. The high school composition program of the future must be planned with this in mind, and nothing less can possibly be accepted as an agreeable substitute.